Coming to Terms with Accession

Forum Report of the Economic Policy Initiative no. 2

Coming to Terms with Accession

Forum Report of the Economic Policy Initiative no. 2

Contributors:

Jürgen von Hagen
Universität Bonn and CEPR

Andrej Kumar
University of Ljubljana

Elżbieta Kawecka-Wyrzykowska
Warsaw School of Economics and Foreign Trade Research Institute, Warsaw

Editors:

Lorand Ambrus-Lakatos
Central European University, Budapest, and CEPR

Mark E. Schaffer
Heriot-Watt University and CEPR

INSTITUTE FOR EASTWEST STUDIES
WARSAW • PRAGUE • BUDAPEST • KOŠICE • NEW YORK

Centre for Economic Policy Research

The Centre for Economic Policy Research is a network of over 300 Research Fellows, based primarily in European universities. The Centre coordinates its Fellows' research activities and communicates their results to the public and private sectors. CEPR is an entrepreneur, developing research initiatives with the producers, consumers and sponsors of research. Established in 1983, CEPR is a European economics research organization with uniquely wide-ranging scope and activities.

CEPR is a registered educational charity. Institutional (core) finance for the Centre is provided by major grants from the Economic and Social Research Council, under which an ESRC Resource Centre operates within CEPR; the Esmée Fairbairn Charitable Trust; the Bank of England; the European Monetary Institute and the Bank for International Settlements; 18 national central banks and 39 companies. None of these organizations gives prior review to the Centre's publications, nor do they necessarily endorse the views expressed therein.

The Centre is pluralist and non-partisan, bringing economic research to bear on the analysis of medium- and long-run policy questions. CEPR research may include views on policy, but the Executive Committee of the Centre does not give prior review to its publications, and the Centre takes no institutional policy positions. The opinions expressed in this report are those of the authors and not those of the Centre for Economic Policy Research.

HC
241.2
.C555
1996

31 October 1996

25–28 Old Burlington Street, London W1X 1LB, UK
Tel: (44 171) 878 2900
Fax: (44 171) 878 2999
Email: cepr@cepr.org

© Economic Policy Initiative, 1996

British Library Cataloguing in Publication Data
A Catalogue record for this book is available from the British Library

ISBN: 1 898128 27 8

Prepared and Printed by MULTIPLEX medway ltd, Walderslade, Kent.

Institute for EastWest Studies (IEWS)

The role of the Institute for EastWest Studies has remained constant since its founding in 1981: to help build a secure, prosperous, democratic, and integrated Europe. It does this as a transatlantic, multinational public policy network and think tank working to assist those who make policy in Europe, Russia, the Newly Independent States, and the United States. It seeks to overcome the divisive legacies of the twentieth century while creating a new order in Europe in which governments, the private sector, and non-governmental organizations work effectively together. The Institute is a non-profit organization, governed by an international Board of Directors and funded by foundations, corporations and individuals from North America, Europe and Japan.

In 1990, the Institute launched a major long-term cooperative venture in Central Europe, with a mandate to sponsor dialogue and cooperative research aimed towards building more secure relationships within and between the East and the West. Its steadily growing presence in the region includes IEWS centres in Prague, Budapest and Warsaw, and the Foundation for the Development of the Carpathian Euroregion (FDCE) in Košice. With direct presence in the United States and Central Europe, liaison offices in other countries of the region and activities conducted in Western Europe as well, the Institute occupies a unique strategic position between East and West.

The Institute's network of political, business and academic associates and its 60 staff in Central Europe and the United States contribute to economic, security and political aspects of IEWS programmes which include: Community Development and Democratic Institutions, European Security, European Integration, and Financial Sector Reform.

Institute for EastWest Studies	IEWS Warsaw Centre
700 Broadway, 2nd Floor	Obożna Street 7/32
New York, NY 10003	00-332 Warsaw
USA	Poland
Tel: (1 212) 824 4100	Tel: (48 22) 268595, 827 0272
Fax: (1 212) 824 4149	Fax: (48 22) 827 0648
President: John E Mroz	Director: Andrzej Rudka
E-mail: iews@iews.org	E-mail: iews@atos.warman.com.pl

Contents

List of Tables

Forum Participants

Vytenis Aleskaitis, *Lithuanian Economic & Foreign Investment Agency (FIDA), Vilnius*
Lorand Ambrus-Lakatos, *Central European University, Budapest, and CEPR*
Graham Avery, *Commission of the European Communities, Brussels*
Vladimir Benacek, *CERGE, Prague*
Jorge Braga de Macedo, *Universidade Nova de Lisboa and CEPR*
László Csaba, *Kopint-Datorg Institute, Budapest*
Janusz M Dabrowski, *Gdańsk Institute for Market Economics*
Renzo Daviddi, *Commission of the European Communities, Brussels*
Rumen Dobrinsky, *21 Century Foundation, Sofia*
Esther Dyson, *EDventure Holdings Inc, New York*
Michael Emerson, *London School of Economics*
László Halpern, *Institute of Economics, Budapest, and CEPR*
Mary Harris, *IEWS, New York*
Stephen Heintz, *IEWS, Prague*
John L Hills, *Commission of the European Communities, Brussels*
Eugen Jurzyca, *Centre for Economic Development (CPHR), Bratislava*
Stefan Kawalec, *Bank Handlowy w Warszawie, Warsaw*
Elżbieta Kawecka-Wyrzykowska, *Warsaw School of Economics and Foreign Trade Research Institute, Warsaw*
Milan Kisztner, *Centre for Economic Development (CPHR), Bratislava*
Jenö Koltay, *Institute of Economics, Budapest*
Andrej Kumar, *University of Ljubljana*
Alan Mayhew, *Katholieke Universiteit Leuven*
Jan Mladek, *Czech Institute of Applied Economics, Prague*
Rolf Moehler, *Commission of the European Communities, Brussels*
Amir Naqvi, *European Commission Delegation, Ljubljana*

Misu Negritoiu, *Romanian Presidency, Bucharest*
Leslaw Paga, *Deloitte & Touche, Warsaw*
Joan Pearce, *Commission of the European Communities, Brussels*
Constanze Picking, *CEPR*
Jaroslaw Pietras, *Bureau for European Integration and Foreign Assistance, Warsaw*
Richard Portes, *London Business School and CEPR*
Janez Prasnikar, *University of Ljubljana*
Ghiorghi Prisacaru, *Secretary of State, Romania*
Gérard Roland, ECARE, *Université Libre de Bruxelles, and CEPR*
Märten Ross, *Bank of Estonia, Tallinn*
Albrecht Rothacher, *Commission of the European Communities, Brussels*
Judit Ròzsa, *Office of the Hungarian Prime Minister, Budapest*
Andrzej Rudka, *IEWS Centre, Warsaw*
André Sapir, ECARE, *Université Libre de Bruxelles, and CEPR*
Mark E Schaffer, *Heriot-Watt University and CEPR*
Brigita Schmögnerová, *Member of Parliament, Slovakia*
Marjan Setinc, *Member of Parliament, Slovenia*
Theodor Stolojan, *World Bank, Washington DC*
Jan Svejnar, *University of Michigan, CERGE-EI, Prague, and CEPR*
Marjan Svetlicic, *University of Ljubljana*
Frantisek Turnovec, *CERGE, Prague*
Stanislaw Uminski, *Gdańsk Institute for Market Economics*
Jürgen von Hagen, *Universität Bonn and CEPR*
Stephen Yeo, *CEPR*
Georgios Zavvos, *European Commission Delegation, Bratislava*

Foreword

Launched towards the end of 1995 by the Centre for Economic Policy Research and the Institute for EastWest Studies, the Economic Policy Initiative comprises a programme of interrelated activities designed to strengthen and 'multilateralize' the public policy process in the Associated Countries (ACs) and assist their preparation for accession to the EU. The Initiative operates in seven EU Associated countries—Bulgaria, the Czech Republic, Hungary, Poland, Romania, the Slovak Republic, and Slovenia— where local partner institutes coordinate activities within their own country. In the first phase of the project, participants from Estonia, Latvia, Lithuania, Russia, and Ukraine are involved as observers.

As part of the Initiative, CEPR and IEWS established the Central European Economic Policy Forum. Here decision-makers from the private sector, senior policy-makers and researchers from both Central and Western Europe meet to discuss key economic policy issues and put forward focused recommendations to the governments of the ACs, the EU and its member states. The Forum meets semi-annually and considers the report of an expert working group, who incorporate into their report the comments and recommendations of the Forum participants for publication. The first Report in the series focused on the presentations of the first Forum on 'Banking Policies in the ACs', held at the College of Europe, Warsaw, in January 1996. A pamphlet containing its main analysis and recommendations and a single-page summary of the proposals is also available. This, the second Report, focuses on presentations of the second Forum on 'Coming to Terms with Accession', held at Université Libre de Bruxelles in June 1996.

We gratefully acknowledge financial support for the Initiative provided by the Ford Foundation, the Pew Charitable Trusts and the EU's Phare Programme. Any opinions expressed in this Report are those of the authors and not those of CEPR, IEWS or the funding organizations. Neither CEPR nor IEWS take institutional policy positions. The funding organizations do not give prior review to the publications within the project, nor do they necessarily endorse the views expressed therein. Lastly, we thank various individuals who have contributed to the success of this project: first and foremost, Constanze Picking and Andrzej Rudka for their energy and determination in the management of the Initiative; Joanna Iwicka and Toni Orloff for their support during the organization of the Forum; James MacGregor for guiding the Report through production; Iwona Ławniczak-Iwanowska and Lorraine Forsdyke for secretarial assistance in the administration of the project; and last, but not least, the authors and editors, whose effort and cooperation in working under a very tight time schedule has been vital.

John Edwin Mroz
Richard Portes
31 October 1996

Introduction

The issue of the accession of the Central and East European (CEE) countries to the European Union (EU) is a contentious one. Perhaps accordingly, this issue of the EPI Forum presents three different perspectives on how the EU, and the CEE countries, should 'come to terms with accession'.

In the first paper, Jürgen von Hagen considers the challenge of accession from the perspective of the EU, and focuses in particular on political economy considerations involved. He begins by noting the importance of security and general political aspects of enlargement but argues that the narrower economic issues will likely move to the centre of the debate as accession negotiations evolve. He then sets out the key features of the political economy calculus of accession for the EU. First of all, the overall economic benefits to the EU are relatively small, but the benefits, and the costs, are unevenly distributed across EU members and across economic sectors. Second, decision-makers in the EU countries and in the European Commission are uncertain about how effectively, and indeed how enthusiastically, the CEE countries can implement EU legislation. Whereas the distributional problem has received much attention, von Hagen points out, the uncertainty problem has been neglected in the debate.

Von Hagen argues that the uncertainty problem creates an option value of postponing enlargement for the EU. Because membership is irreversible, immediately granting membership to countries and then discovering that they were either unable or unwilling to implement the Single European Market would be very costly to the current EU members. Postponing enlargement would reduce the uncertainty; hence the option value of waiting.

Von Hagen suggests that the distributional problem and the uncertainty problem require different policy responses to facilitate timely enlargement. If the distributional issue is regarded as the principal problem, each CEE country should develop its own accession strategy trying to speed up approximation of its legal system to EU law and limiting participation to those areas where the distributional problems are not too large.

Solving the uncertainty problem, in contrast, requires a much different approach. What is necessary is for the CEE countries to build the credibility of their commitments to establishing market economies in general, and of their intentions to pass and implement effectively EU legislation in particular. Regional cooperation within CEE, suggests von Hagen, is one way in which the credibility of the CEE countries can be enhanced and the accession process facilitated. At the same time, reducing the risk of negative externalities to existing EU members of allowing in countries prematurely would make entry more attractive to them. One way this could be done would be to give the EU the possibility, following the initial accession, to respond to non-compliance by a new CEE member with EU product standards or competition laws by imposing trade barriers against the new member. Von Hagen proposes the creation of a new institution, the Accession Council, in which the EU and the CEE countries would be represented, and which would be vested with the authority to impose such measures.

The second author, Andrej Kumar, places the issue of enlargement in a larger context. He argues that it is not the accession to the EU which ought to be the primary aspiration of the CEE countries, but 'catching up' with the most developed economies in the world. The real question is whether the enlargement of the EU could contribute to these efforts or not, and whether in its absence there would be any chance left for the CEE countries to raise substantially their levels of economic development. Kumar cites the example of the so-called 'Asian Tigers', emphasizing the fact that they narrowed the development gap without having to join an Asian equivalent of the EU or anything similar. He also mentions that the most important indicator of past success with integration seems to be the convergence of the development level of the partners involved.

Kumar covers a number of very important analytical questions in his paper, including the role of public opinion in the assessment of the motivations of the Eastern partners, and also the problems surrounding the measurement of economic growth in the region. He lists the options which the CEE countries face with respect to economic integration, and also the options which the EU has with respect to the form in which the process of enlargement could take place.

Kumar concludes that both of the two European regions would benefit significantly from a well-organized accession process. The EU cannot afford to enter into the next phase of global competition without integrating the CEE countries. For the latter, accession to the EU provides the best opportunity to modernize their economies and approach at least the average level of development in the current EU. All this requires that the EU announce clear and attainable criteria in the near future which the CEE countries have to fulfill in order to gain membership. This, of course, presupposes that these accession criteria are not used as a 'barrier to entry' and that the EU persists in seeking a clear evaluation of the costs and benefits of enlargement.

The third author, Elżbieta Kawecka-Wyrzykowska, bases her arguments on two foundations. The first of these is that the enlargement of the EU, by creating a larger common market, is beneficial both for the current members of the EU and for the CEE countries. At the same time, there are overwhelming political and security reasons for the incorporation of the Eastern countries as well; only this can assure a stable and safe Europe in the future.

Assessing the endeavor to integrate the CEE countries, she detects signs of hesitation and ambivalence on the part of EU leaders. She offers refutations to many arguments which oppose granting full membership to some of the CEE countries in the near future. Accordingly, she points to exaggerations in some claims about the difficulties in dealing with CEE agriculture in the EU. Kawecka-Wyrzykowska also criticizes the view that the EU would have to transfer too many resources to the CEE countries through the structural funds; current EU rules should not be used for the assessment of future costs of the integration. In her view, the EU White Paper suggests unreasonably stringent conditions for the accession, omits some crucial issues, and avoids the announcement of a transparent and well-crafted agenda for the integration process.

Kawecka-Wyrzykowska concludes that there is no strong argument against the inclusion of the CEE countries into the EU, very soon and as full members. If this was for some reason not to happen, then the Eastern economies would lose their potential for any possible integration. This would also destabilize their economic policy-making. In turn, Europe as a whole would have to face a dangerous situation.

Lorand Ambrus-Lakatos
Mark E. Schaffer

1

The Political Economy of Eastern Enlargement of the EU*

Jürgen von Hagen

University of Bonn, Indiana University, and CEPR

1.1   Introduction

For more than four decades, the countries of Central and Eastern Europe had to live under the umbrella of Soviet domination. The socialist regime imposed an almost complete severance of the traditional economic, political and cultural links between the region and its Western neighbours and transformed the economies into central planning regimes. When the Central and East European (CEE) countries expressed their interest in joining the European Communities immediately after the opening-up of the region in the late 1980s and early 1990s, their bid for membership was welcomed by the European Union (EU) as a signal of their commitment to the transition to market economies and Western-style democracy.

Now that the initial euphoria is over, the views and sentiments about integration of the region into the EU have become more sober and realistic. Transformation has turned out to be more difficult, both economically and politically, than it was perceived at the beginning. Closer cooperation with the EU has started in the form of various programmes for assistance, but the Union has been very reluctant to enter into any commitments regarding the timing or strategy of an eastern enlargement other than the promise that accession talks will start within six months after the end of the current Intergovernmental Conference (IGC). This has spurred disappointment in the region, where the EU is now sometimes seen as a 'big bully' rather than a sympathetic neighbour (Drabek, 1995). Misunderstanding of the terms of accession on both sides risk spoiling the climate of cooperation.

This paper studies the political economy of the eastern enlargement from the perspective of the EU. In section 1.2, we begin with characterizing the political and economic interests involved, i.e., the expected benefits and the costs at the level of the Union, the individual member states and the various economic sectors. While the aggregate benefits from enlargement are rather small for the EU, the distribution of the expected costs and benefits among the members is quite uneven. The prospect of enlargement, therefore, creates distributional problems within the current EU. The distributional difficulties are augmented by the development gap, i.e., the fact that the economies are in very different stages of development from EU economies, the possibility that enlargement leads to negative externalities in addition to positive ones, and the potential participation of the newcomers in transfer mechanisms within the EU that were designed to solve earlier distribution problems. Furthermore, the eastern enlargement involves a large degree of uncertainty about the capacity and willingness of the candidate countries to implement EU legislation. This is due to the lack of a track record with market-oriented policies and an institutional environment in the transition economies that is still in the process of transformation. The Commission in particular must be concerned about the risks enlargement creates for the proper functioning of the Single Market.

In Section 1.3 we analyze the bargaining problems between the EU and the CEE countries. Earlier studies of the enlargement problem have focused almost exclusively on the distributional issues. In contrast, the problem of uncertainty has not yet received the full attention it deserves, although its consequences are clearly visible in the EU's and, particularly, the European Commission's position regarding enlargement. The characteristics of the problem, a large initial investment in the form of the property rights connected with membership, the non-reversibility of membership which makes this investment a sunk cost, and uncertain future pay-offs which, over time, are more likely to increase than to decrease, imply that postponement of enlargement has a positive option value: it allows the incumbents to reduce uncertainty and improves the chances, from their perspective, that enlargement will eventually be beneficial and cause limited costs.

Distinguishing the distributional from the uncertainty problem is essential, because the two have very different implications regarding the development of an enlargement strategy. We discuss the strategic implications of the two dimensions in Section 1.4. Strategy proposals aimed at solving the distributional problems generally point in the direction of graded membership, i.e., allowing the candidates to participate in all aspects of the European Union that do not imply large-scale transfers of resources. Strategies developed from the perspective of the distributional issues emphasize country and sector-specific solutions and the importance of striking a proper balance between limiting the degree of EU membership to reduce the distributional implications and the potential deterioration of the enlargement process into cherry-picking only the most convenient parts of EU membership. In contrast, a strategy developed from the perspective of the uncertainty problem emphasizes the importance of building credibility of the CEE countries' commitment to market economies and their willingness and ability to implement the Single European Market. Building a market-oriented institutional framework and a track record of market-oriented policies are key elements in such a strategy. Regional cooperation can play a large role here as a way to signal the readiness of the candidate countries to become members.

Recognizing the uncertainty problem is not in itself a justification for delaying enlargement and emphasizing the importance of the option-value of waiting is not the same as advocating postponement of the eastern enlargement. We emphasize this rather obvious point to avoid misunderstanding. Importantly, however, failure to understand the relevance of the uncertainty problem may easily become a reason for a protracted accession process. By describing the problem and its strategic implications, our hope is to facilitate a timely accession of the CEE countries to the EU.

Eastern enlargement cannot be seen as an economic project alone. From the EU's perspective, it also has a broad, (geo-)political dimension. Bringing the CEE countries out of the sphere of Russian dominance is obviously a most important element; promoting peace and democratic stability at the eastern border of the Union is equally important. Failure to develop close links with the CEE countries might carry a large price in terms of political unrest in the region and the necessity to maintain sizeable military and security forces to protect the Union against the spillovers of such instabilities. Thus, the eastern enlargement carries with it a kind of *peace dividend*. The political dimension was very clearly expressed at the Copenhagen Summit, which acknowledged the CEE countries' prospects of becoming members and included democratic government and acknowledgement of the principles of international cooperation in Europe among the conditions for entry.

Nevertheless, it would be equally foolish to sweep away all economic considerations with a broad allusion to the political importance of the Eastern enlargement for the EU. In fact, the importance of the general political considerations for the enlargement process is hard to judge and unlikely to remain a constant throughout the process. On the one hand, their weight will depend on the course of political events in Russia and in the region itself: should democracy and economic reform lose out in Russia, the EU's readiness for a rapid enlargement would probably increase quickly. But if that does not happen, the narrower economic issues will tend to move to the centre as the enlargement process proceeds.

Furthermore, the political interest in enlargement is not the same throughout the Union. Not surprisingly, Germany has pushed most strongly for the eastern enlargement. Germany's position in this matter reflects its position at the current eastern border of the EU and the tragic memories of its historical role as a country finding itself caught in the 'middle position' between the political interests of the East and the West (CDU, 1994). From Germany's perspective, Eastern enlargement of the EU is an essential element of peaceful stability in

Europe. Sweden supports the Baltic bid for accession for similarly geographical interests. But the political desire for eastern enlargement also meets opposition. France has historically supported European integration in the hope of remaining a dominant European power, while at the same time keeping Germany firmly tied to a Western political and military alliance.[1] Close integration with the CEE countries would dilute the influence of France and shift the political balance of the Union towards the East. The prospect of such a shift may have prompted President Mitterrand to declare that it would take 'decades and decades' before membership of the CEE countries could be considered (Pinder, 1994).[2] With this in mind, the remainder of this paper focuses on the economic policy problems.

1.2   EU Expectations and Concerns Regarding Enlargement

To identify the EU's expectations and concerns regarding the economic policy aspects of enlargement, it helps to characterize the relations between the Union and the CEE countries as a two-level game. The characteristic of such games is that the players in the international negotiations (the Commission in our case) have to resolve simultaneous internal conflicts among the members (Putnam, 1988; Guggenbuehl, 1995). The responses to the opponent in the international negotiations, therefore, depend on how conflicts are resolved within the Union as well as on the conflicts between the Union as an aggregate body and the CEE countries.

At the level of the member states, there are different political and economic interests, some in favour and some against accession. Apart from threatening existing economic interests, the enlargement is seen as an obstacle for deepening European integration among the current members—a factor which some members regard as more important. For the same reason, those members who do not wish to proceed with deeper integration favour enlargement as a strategy slowing down the process of integration.

At the level of the Commission, the interest in enlargement is equally divided. On the one hand, the economic theory of bureaucracies suggests that the Commission should favour enlargement as a strategy to increase the territorial domain of its own jurisdiction: in a larger Union, the role and political importance of the Commission will be greater. For a similar reason, however, the Commission must be interested in deepening European integration as a strategy to increase the functional domain of its authority. To the extent that enlargement makes greater integration more difficult, the Commission might opt for the latter rather than the former. At the same time, the Commission must be interested in preserving the proper functioning of the existing institutions since any disturbance in that area might be regarded as failure on the part of the Commission.

1.2.1 Member State Interests

General Trade Issues

The economic opening up of Central and Eastern Europe initially raised much concern about the danger of low-cost competition from these countries. Since then, there seems to be a growing consensus that the initial pessimism was not justified. Trade between the EU and the CEE countries has grown fairly rapidly and without causing major structural disturbances. In the five years from 1989 to 1993, imports from the CEE countries to the EU grew by an average annual rate of 15.9%; the strongest growth performance was in machinery and transport equipment and other manufactured articles. Exports from the EU to the CEE countries grew by an average rate of 23.6% in the same period, with the strongest performance in mineral fuels and again machinery, transport equipment and other manufactures (Faini and Portes, 1995). Trade growth between the EU and the CEE countries by far exceeded the growth of trade between the EU and other trading partners.[3]

The Europe Agreements (and the Interim Agreements signed to speed up the establishment of new trade relations) stipulate the trade regime between the CEE countries and the EU. They abolish tariffs and quantitative restrictions on all industrial products not included in exceptions. Nevertheless, they represent a smaller step towards free trade than they might seem at first glance. Beyond some basic products (mostly minerals and leather), exceptions were made for 'sensitive products', the list of which varies between the CEE countries and clearly reflects successful protectionist pressures resulting from sectoral interests in the member states. According to Gabrisch (1995), the share of EU imports of restricted goods from the CEE countries fell from 41.3% in 1990 to 37.6% in 1993. Restricted products thus still represent an important part of the EU-CEE trade.

In light of the fact that the current production and trade patterns of the CEE countries are still heavily distorted by direct, pre-1989 government interventions in the economy, it is hard to predict today the patterns of trade and comparative advantages between the region and the EU that will develop over time (Faini and Portes, 1995). The rapid growth of EU-CEE trade probably reflects unused exchange opportunities under the old regime and excess capacities in the transition process more than a swift move towards a new trade equilibrium. This is consistent with the observation that the commodity structure of CEE exports changed only slightly in the first four years after their opening to the West.[4] The heavy industrial restructuring in East Germany since 1990 suggests that adjustment to world market relative prices requires very large changes in production patterns (von Hagen, 1995; Hare, 1994). The full benefits from EU-CEE trade—for both sides—will develop only gradually over time, as the old distortions are corrected. In the short run, the benefits of these developments will be overshadowed by the pressures for import protection by the sectors exposed to new competition.

In fact, all Europe Agreements allow for contingent protection, i.e., the reintroduction of trade barriers when import competition leads to sectoral disturbances. With rather undefined conditionalities, there is much room for discretion on the part of the EU. Although such measures have to be discussed with the CEE country concerned, they can be imposed unilaterally if agreement has not been reached within 30 days in the Association Council. As a result, the stability of the new trade regime remains uncertain.[5]

Studies of the long-run output, employment, and welfare effects of increased CEE-EU trade in the EU commonly conclude that the overall impact will remain relatively small. Given the small initial base effects, trade would remain small even if it multiplied several times (Gasiorek et al., 1994). Dittus and Anderson (1995) estimate a reduction of aggregate European employment by up to 0.5% due to increased imports from the CEE countries, and reductions of between 0.4% and 1.3% of sectoral employment in the sensitive industries.[6] These changes would be small relative to the reduction of employment in the same sectors during the 1980s (2.2% total). Similar results are found in studies of the effects of increased CEE trade on output and welfare (Gasiorek et al., 1994; Rollo and Smith, 1993), which indicate noticeable losses of producer surplus in some EU industries, but large increases in consumer surplus due to lower goods prices.

Overall, these results suggest that the aggregate benefits of trade integration with the CEE countries will be positive, though small. The distribution of these benefits, however, will differ significantly across different sectors of the EU economies and between producers and consumers. The resulting distributional problems will shape the political economy of the accession process.

National Trade Interests

As European decision-making involves national governments and the Commission, one must consider country-specific differences in such sectoral effects. Padoan and Pericoli (1993) and De Benedictis and Padoan (1994) use the measurement of revealed comparative advantage to pin down these differences. They suggest that Germany, the UK and France have clear comparative advantages over the CEE countries in science-based industries, industries with strong economies of scale and industries relying on specialized suppliers. In contrast, the CEE countries have comparative advantages in traditional industries, resource-intensive and energy-intensive industries. Italy, Spain, Portugal and Greece share the competitive disadvantage in science-based and scale-intensive industries and the advantage in traditional industries. Thus, increased trade with the CEE countries would expose the Southern Europeans to fiercer competition, while the Northern Europeans would benefit. Padoan and Pericoli (1993) point out that the Southern European countries are also under the greatest pressure to adjust to the Single

Market. This will increase their reluctance to admit new countries to the Union. One should note, however, that the concept of revealed comparative advantage is heavily biased by historical distortions in the CEE economies. Gasiorek et al. (1994), who use a more detailed, calibrated trade model, conclude that adverse regional effects of increased CEE exports to the EU would be limited. Nevertheless, there is a significant danger that sectoral interests show up as conflicts of interest between EU member states and that this makes the enlargement process more difficult.

Agriculture

So far, trade policies vis-à-vis the CEE countries have barely touched barriers to trade in agricultural products, although (or because?) farming provides major export opportunities. Begg et al. (1990) and Hamilton and Winters (1992) estimate that farming output could increase by at least 40% as a consequence of the economic restructuring of the CEE economies. Based on that estimate, the CEE countries would become significant net exporters of grains and livestock (Baldwin et al., 1992). Access to EU agricultural markets would mean relatively high prices for CEE farmers, contributing to the incentive to increase output.

Under the Europe Agreements, tariffs and variable levies on agricultural products are to be reduced but not eliminated. Relatively minor import quotas in agricultural products have been all the CEE countries could obtain in this area so far.[7] The main obstacle to liberalizing trade in agricultural products is, of course, the Union's Common Agricultural Policy (CAP). That a reform of the CAP is long overdue is no secret in Europe. There is widespread agreement among European economists that such reform should separate its efficient part—free trade in agricultural products—from the inefficient part—the use of price support mechanisms to support farming incomes (Dewatripont et al., 1995). This is not to deny that income support for farmers may be desirable. Yet, the combination of price and income support results in prices far exceeding world market prices, excessive production within the EU combined with inefficient use of fertilizers and pesticides, and high trade barriers against outsiders. Separating income support from price support, however, would make the actual benefits for the farmers directly visible to the public and, therefore, focus political opposition against a system that benefits only a small group at the cost of the majority of society. A move to direct income support would thus raise the farmers' risk of losing their subsidies altogether.

The enormous political clout of farmers' organizations, such as those in Germany, has so far prevented reform of the CAP. Linking CAP reform to eastern enlargement or relying on it as a condition for enlargement are, therefore, sure recipes for postponing enlargement. Without CAP reform, liberalizing trade in agricultural products with the CEE countries could take two routes. One would be a full-fledged participation of CEE farmers in the CAP. Given the relatively low farming incomes and prices in the CEE countries, this would result in a huge increase in CAP-related spending (Baldwin, 1994). Either the entire EU budget would be spent on the CAP—an outcome opposed by those who benefit from other EU—or the budget would have to be increased—a result net contributors would oppose.

The alternative would be to let CEE farmers participate in EU agricultural trade in exchange for foregoing any CAP benefits. But this is equally non-viable from a politico-economic perspective. If low-price CEE products drive EU products out of the market, CAP subsidies would have to rise to maintain farming incomes. At the same time, the EU public would understand that low-cost supply of agricultural products to the Union is feasible, i.e., the income-support side of the CAP would become more visible. Anticipating these factors would incite political opposition to even a limited CEE participation in the CAP.

Services

Trade liberalization in services remains limited to cross-border provision of services rendered by employees who are nationals of the importing countries. There are no clear rules for mutual recognition of diploma and professional certification, reflecting the large differences in educational systems. Since the financial services industries in the CEE countries are still in the process of reconstruction and are affected by structural problems and non-performing loans, it is not surprising that the Europe Agreements make no room for integrating the financial markets. Banking technology is generally not up to West European standards. Banking regulation in such an environment poses problems very different to the regulation of EU banks and demands different regulatory approaches (Tirole, 1994), making the EU approach of home-country regulation and mutual recognition inapplicable.

Factor Mobility

Capital mobility remains limited between the EU and the CEE countries. The Europe Agreements provide that payments can be made in convertible currencies as long as they are related to trade and the movement of persons. Capital mobility is also limited to direct investment, for which the repatriation of capital and profits are guaranteed within five years of the initial investment. The Agreements also provide for a commitment not to introduce new foreign exchange restrictions between the CEE countries and the EU within five years.

Labour mobility remains limited to the non-discrimination of persons legally residing in the EU. Since migration policies regarding non-EU citizens remain the domain of national policies, the Agreements did not establish a common policy in this area. West European incentives regarding migration are ambivalent. On the one hand, there is the fear that migrant CEE workers, attracted by much higher wages and more generous social protection in the EU, would displace domestic workers and cause an already excessive unemployment in Europe to increase further. Labour unions, particularly in Germany, will oppose migration strongly, fearing that it would undermine the stability of labour market cartels delivering high wages and job security to their members.[8] On the other hand, several European countries, including Germany, suffer from severe ageing problems which undermine the sustainability of their social security systems. A significant inflow of younger workers from the East, who would contribute to the social security systems for a long period before drawing retirement benefits, could help to spread out the adjustment of these systems over time. This creates some basis for a favourable view of migration in rapidly ageing countries such as Germany and Italy (Hoffmann, 1995).

Incentives for migration are largely influenced by expectations.[9] What matters is not simply the current wage differential between two regions, but the difference in expected future incomes properly discounted, which accounts for employment probabilities and expected wages at home. Since rising exports promise job creation and rising wages, a liberal EU trade regime towards the CEE countries is, to some extent at least, a substitute for a liberal migration policy. Baldwin et al. (1992) estimate that a liberal trade regime with the EU could increase the demand for labour in the CEE countries by 6% to 10%. Similar suggestions come from empirical studies of the effects on employment of trade based on comparative advantage (Bowen et al., 1987). A liberal trade regime could thus reduce the incentive for migration.

The practical difficulty with that proposition is that the incentives within the EU are not distributed in a way that encourages the use of this substitutability. Specifically, those countries that fear CEE competition the most—Spain, Portugal, Greece and Italy—also fear migration the least, since their wage differentials with the CEE countries are much smaller. A proposal for trade concessions in return for restrictive migration practices would be supported by the northern EU members but meet opposition from the southern EU countries.

1.2.2   Budgetary Issues

Budgetary implications of CEE country membership in the EU have received much attention in recent years. Most commentators are concerned with the potential effects of full CEE country membership on the Union's income redistribution policies, the CAP, structural funds and regional funds. Given their low GDPs in comparison to the EU countries (the 1991 average per capita GDP in the Visegrad states was about one third of the EU-12 average—Baldwin, 1994), all CEE countries would be net beneficiaries from these funds unless the rules for distribution were changed markedly.

Baldwin et al. (1992) find that the distribution of structural funds among the current EU members can be explained by their per capita income levels and the share of agriculture in GDP. Since the CEE countries rank relatively low on the former and high on the latter scale, their estimated receipts would amount to almost the entire sum available for structural funds in the EU budget for 1990. Payments under the CAP to these countries would amount to roughly 14% of the amount budgeted for this purpose in 1990. Focusing on the Visegrad states, Anderson and Tyers (1993) estimate that CAP spending would increase by ECU 37.6 billion and structural funds spending by ECU 26 billion, if these countries were admitted in the year 2000. Courchene et al. (1993) estimate that the Visegrad states would receive ECU 26 billion in structural funds by the year 2000. Re-estimating his earlier model for 1991, Baldwin (1994) puts a total budget cost of admitting the Visegrad states at ECU 11 billion.

CEE participation in these programmes raises two possibilities. First, the EU could respond by changing the regional structure of its expenditure without changing the total amount, making participation a zero-sum game. This would turn the current net recipients of funds—Greece, Spain, Portugal, and Ireland—into net contributors and raise their opposition against enlargement. Second, the EU could increase its total budget to make room for the additional expenditure. Using the estimates from Baldwin et al. (1992), this would require an increase of 31% in the EU budget for 1990. Assuming that the pattern of contributions would remain roughly the same, this would raise the opposition of the current net contributors—Belgium, Germany, France, Italy and the UK. Thus, although the total budgetary implications amount to only a third of 1% of the combined 1990 GDP of member states, the distributional aspect raises opposition. Finally, the different cost implications of admitting different countries to the EU as suggested by Baldwin (1994) create an incentive for the Commission to pick the 'low-cost' countries first for enlargement and keep the 'high-cost' countries waiting in line.

1.2.3   Monetary Union

Subscribing to full EU membership raises the question whether the CEE countries must accept the project of monetary union. In the original negotiations leading to the Maastricht Treaty, only Britain and Denmark obtained the right to stay out of monetary union if they so wished at the start. Sweden was granted the option of staying out of monetary union after its accession to the Union. Germany's supreme court ruled that the German parliament could not be bound by a European Council decision in a matter so far-reaching several years before it was taken and without knowing what the outcome would be. Germany, therefore, ratified the Maastricht Treaty only conditionally and the German parliament will have a final vote on the matter at the scheduled start of monetary union.

All these observations suggest that participating in monetary union is not necessarily required of the CEE countries. One may expect that the Commission will insist on their acceptance of monetary union, since the EU would otherwise have a sizeable group of members with derogations from monetary union, which would make their status seem much less exceptional than it currently does. But this may be exactly the reason why some members with less interest in monetary union might support the wish of the CEE countries to stay out of monetary union. In the more political forum of the European Council, the CEE countries could then play the card of a timely accession against the requirement of participation in monetary union.

From the perspective of the incumbent members, CEE country participation in monetary union requires a sufficiently high degree of macroeconomic stability in these countries. The debate on whether macroeconomic convergence should come before or as a result of monetary union has a long tradition in the EU (Fratianni and von Hagen, 1992). The compromise reached in the Maastricht Treaty regarding this debate can be seen in the formulation of convergence criteria, numerical limits for inflation, interest rates, general government deficits and debt, and the requirement that exchange rates fluctuate within the normal boundaries of the European Monetary System for at least two years. As the CEE countries still seem quite far from meeting these requirements, making monetary union a binding requirement would delay enlargement. At the same time, the policy mix required to achieve the fiscal and monetary criteria for monetary union would likely slow down economic growth in the transition economies and thus prolong the reform process required for accession (Coricelli, 1996).

1.2.4   The Commission's Position

As indicated above, one should expect that the Commission's attitude towards eastward enlargement of the EU is mixed. Enlargement raises the Commission's prospect of becoming a more powerful institution given its larger territorial domain. It also could slow down the pace of the integration process among the current members and thus hinder the growing authority of the Commission from that perspective. Finally, enlargement is risky from the Commission's point of view, since any disturbance to the proper working of the EU could lead to a public perception that the Commission has not lived up to its challenges.

Although it was prepared under extreme time pressure and not with the purpose of developing a detailed strategy for enlargement, the Commission's White Paper (Commission 1995) is a natural source from which it is possible to glean its position on the relevant issues. First, the Paper lays out a strategy for convergence of the CEE countries to the Single Market, emphasizing that convergence towards the Single Market is not the same as moving closer to accession to the Union. Adopting Single Market membership would not require the CEE countries to adopt the legislation of the EU (the *acquis communautaire*) in all aspects. This suggests that the Commission envisions an enlargement of the Single Market earlier than enlargement of the European Union.

Second, the Commission did not want to commit itself to automatic membership, even if the CEE countries fulfil all the requirements for participating in the Single Market. By avoiding such a commitment, the EU retains the initiative, giving the Commission more influence on the eventual timing and modalities of accession. Third, the White Paper argues that preparing the CEE countries for the Single Market is essential to safeguard the smooth functioning of the Single Market for the benefit of all members after accession. This suggests that the Commission fears the blame for disturbances in the working of the Single Market more than it cherishes its payoff from enlargement. This is in line with the proposition in the White Paper, namely that preparation for the Single Market is primarily the responsibility of the CEE countries. Fourth, the White Paper's organizing logic is to spell out requirements for each economic sector, reflecting the organization of the Commission itself. Although this may be a result of time pressure, the lack of coordination of the requirements across sectors might indicate that the Commission is unwilling to accept compromises across different sectors. Such an approach would maximize rigidity and makes the success of the project dependent on the slowest part.

Fifth, the White Paper draws up a list of requirements much larger than those formulated in earlier accessions. One way of interpreting this is that the White Paper reflects the extent of influence of EU sectoral interests on the Commission (Smith et al., 1996), i.e., that the Commission was dominated by internal, distributional conflicts within the EU. If this is the case, involving the political organs of the Union more strongly would facilitate the accession process.

Another interpretation can be drawn from the observation that the Commission faces a large degree of informational uncertainty regarding the reliable implementation in the CEE countries of the requirements for accession. This uncertainty simply reflects the fact that the Commission has no experience in dealing with transition economies, and that the political and economic systems in these countries are still too much in flux to make reliable predictions about their behaviour. As a result, the Commission may have taken the view that increasing the number of requirements to be imposed on the CEE countries prior to negotiations on accession reduces the threat of destabilization in the incumbent EU following enlargement, even if each requirement is implemented only insufficiently. Of course, this ignores the possibility that proper implementation of a few rules might produce a better outcome than poor implementation of many, and the fact that the CEE countries' inadequate administrative resources mean this tradeoff must be faced.

With its mandate to administer the working of the Single Market, the Commission must be particularly concerned with competition and trade policies in the CEE countries. We now turn to a review of these areas to illustrate the difficulties the Commission faces.

Competition Policy

Competition policy in the EU aims at limiting market power to guarantee the proper working of competitive market forces. Specifically, it intends to preserve open markets and facilitate integration of national markets by controlling the abuse and the emergence of market power. Competition policy includes actions against monopolies, merger control, the abuse of dominant firm positions, and collusive behaviour (see e.g., Cave and Estrin, 1994). Even in established market economies, implementing competition policy faces a dilemma, because it is often hard to demonstrate that a specific business action or practice caused economic harm.

The Europe Agreements mandate the establishment of competition policies in the association states. This follows from the requirement of GATT rules which allow the creation of regional free trade arrangements only if trade is governed by competition (Kuschel, 1995). But the Europe Agreements and the White Paper have gone further and asked the CEE countries to approximate their competition policies to the EU's policies. Even before that has happened, EU law must be applied in the association states.

At a formal level, approximation involves the passing of competition laws resembling current EU legislation and the creation of authorities charged with their implementation. Competition legislation has been passed in all CEE countries in recent years, but the legislation in Poland, Romania and Slovakia must still be considered incomplete.[10] Authorities charged explicitly with the implementation of competition policies have been created in Poland, Slovakia, Slovenia, the Czech Republic and Hungary. Fingleton et al. (1996), after reviewing competition laws in the Visegrad countries, conclude that formal approximation has already reached a high degree despite visible differences in the wording of pertinent national legislation.

One must realize, however, that the purposes of competition policy in the EU and in transition economies cannot be the same: in the EU it aims at strengthening competition in compartmentalized national markets; in transition economies it is aimed at breaking up market power inherited from the pre-transition regimes (de la Laurencie, 1994). Slay (1995) reports that the competition authorities in Hungary and Poland were actively involved in the privatization process, but that competition policy as defined in the EU plays only a minor role in the reduction of market power in these economies. Even with close formal approximation, the practice of competition policy will be different in the two regions. Fingleton et al. (1996) indicate that CEE competition laws put more emphasis on concepts of fairness as a goal of competition policies than EU legislation. Thiel's (1995) review of cartel and competition legislation in a larger sample of states comes to a similar conclusion. Thiel combines his findings with a sobering warning against relying too strongly on formal approximation: the lack of established judicial practice and, in fact, of sufficient legal infrastructure, still leaves a great deal of legal uncertainty in the CEE countries regarding competition policies.

All CEE economies are characterized by industrial restructuring at both the sectoral and the firm level. At the sectoral level, resources should move from non-competitive to competitive sectors. Economic theory argues that this should take place in a process of creation and destruction of monopolies. Thus, it is not clear that the application of standards and methods of competition policy that are suitable for markets in equilibrium is adequate or desirable in economies of transition. On the one hand, the basic approach to competition policy is to regulate the behaviour of firms already operating in a market. US experience with antitrust policies (Feinberg and Meurs, 1994) suggests that this approach is much less promising than the alternative, namely to promote entry of new competitors into the market. Given that both competition policy and entry promotion demand sizeable administrative resources, there is a clear danger that by focusing too much on the former, too little is done to promote entry, such as fighting against pressure groups favouring restrictive trade policies and other barriers to entry. In the worst case, competition policy in the transition economies risks deteriorating into bureaucratic management of highly monopolized or cartelized markets.

On the other hand, stringent competition policies against monopolies, for example, might hinder the restructuring processes necessary for a successful transition to market economies. Fornalcyk (1994) notes that competition policy is often in conflict with the actions and policies required by government programmes for restructuring the Polish economy. Thiel (1995) points out that foreign investors will often find that the firms they invest in have inherited a dominant market position from the past, and that the influx of foreign capital will tend to strengthen that position. A stringent application of competition laws might drive foreign capital away from such investments and, thereby, contribute to the current capital shortage. Furthermore, government intervention for the sake of competition policy is commonly based on observed market structure, observed business conduct, or economic performance (Estrin and Cave, 1994). It can, therefore, only be based on past behaviour of markets and firms. Yet, in rapidly changing markets, past behaviour may not be strongly correlated to present or future behaviour. Thus, the risk of inadequate actions is higher than in markets in equilibrium (Fingleton et al., 1996).

The implications of this are two-fold. First, the CEE countries' interest in speedy policy convergence towards EU practice is rather limited. Second, even if an active competition policy is deemed desirable, it will likely take forms quite different from current EU policies. This, however, implies that the adequacy of CEE countries' policies in this domain will remain hard to judge from the EU's perspective. This problem is accentuated by the fact that, in contrast to EU legislation (Commission Regulation 17/62), national competition laws in the Visegrad states do not treat procedural aspects in detail (de la Laurencie, 1994), thus leaving an impression of arbitrariness and increasing uncertainty about the quality of the implementation of competition law.

Evidence from the relevant case law in the Visegrad countries (Fingleton et al., 1996) confirms these considerations. On the one hand, the case law has placed much greater emphasis on abuse of dominance than on other market imperfections. Authorities were often willing to presume the existence of dominance based on very simple and questionable indicators such as concentration in the market relevant for the plaintiff party, rather than the potential market of the defendant, and that dominance was sufficient proof of abuse. On the other hand, too few resources have been invested in the regulation of other forms of uncompetitive practice, specifically cartels. Finally, a tendency seems to exist in merger control whereby exemption rules are used for purposes of industrial policy. Merger control has tended to be quite lax if the merger strengthened the position of domestic firms relative to foreign firms. While this is, of course, not unheard of in EU member states, it creates conflicts with trade policies and indicates a willingness to give industrial policy considerations precedence over competition policy.

The report by Fingleton et al. (1996) suggests that, except in network industries such as energy and telecommunications, where regulatory policies remain undeveloped, state-owned firms are not formally sheltered from competition legislation in the Visegrad states. In practice, however, it is not clear to what extent state-owned companies are subject to the same rules as private businesses. While the competition authorities were quite effective in breaking up large companies prior to privatization in Poland, the same is apparently not true in the other Visegrad states. State aid generally does not come under the jurisdiction of competition authorities. Similarly, competition authorities play a fairly restricted role in decisions involving conflicts between trade policies and competition policy and the latter and industrial policy, although in some countries they are formally involved in the decision-making process. Overall, Fingleton et al. characterize the authorities as (1) having little control over state activities affecting competition, (2) weak in dealing with state-owned enterprises, (3) not sufficiently independent from their national governments. In economies emerging from a system of state control, this suggests that the relevant institutions are ineffective.

Restructuring at company level occurs mainly in the form of downsizing existing, large state-owned companies during or after privatization. Empirical evidence reviewed in Fingleton et al. (1996) suggests that labour-shedding has been dramatic, but bankruptcy rates have been rather low. In the four Visegrad states, the evidence suggests that the shares of large firms in manufacturing output or employment remains large. Carlin et al. (1994) report several cases in which dominant firms in Poland and Hungary used their strategic advantages to drive competitors out of their markets. In addition, lax policies towards tax and social security legislation (OECD, 1994a) have allowed firms to maintain soft budget constraints. Fingleton et al. and the OECD (1995) report similar evidence from Hungary. According to the OECD (1994b), lax enforcement of the new bankruptcy law and permissive loan policies of the— still largely state-owned—banks have allowed poorly-performing companies in the Czech Republic to remain in business. Such practices create competitive distortions favouring mainly large, poorly-performing state-owned enterprises. It is clear that the prevalence of such indirect state aid creates substantial uncertainties about the implementation of competition policies for outsiders such as the EU, leading to the presumption that anti-competitive practices are more widespread than 'official' government policies might suggest. Thus, Drabek (1994) claims that budgetary state aid in the Czech Republic was strongly reduced in recent years and complains that the EU has not honoured these efforts sufficiently. The Commission's rebuttal is that even though the Czechs may be truly advanced in their market reform, the elimination of production subsidies is not sufficient. Instead, the real problem is the absence of 'market culture' (Drabek 1994, p. 144). While Drabek takes this as a sign of the Commission's unfriendly behaviour towards the CEE countries, it may simply reflect its hesitancy to make early concessions to a partner whose true practices are difficult to assess.

Apart from the volume of restructuring, the quality of restructuring is also important: industries in transition must move towards structures that enable them to survive under market conditions in the long run. Evidence presented in Grosfeld and Roland (1995) and Carlin et al. (1994) suggests that a majority of firms in the Visegrad countries has so far shied away from strategic restructuring, i.e., the development of a consistent business strategy. This suggests that the current restructuring processes do not move the CEE economies closer to a position where reliable implementation of competition policies similar to those in the EU can be expected.

According to a common argument in the early debate on transformation, granting market access to foreign companies would provide sufficient competitive pressure to force domestic industries to restructure themselves into competitive positions. The evidence available so far (Grosfeld and Roland, 1995; Carlin et al., 1994) suggests that this has happened sometimes, but not always. Strategic restructuring occurred almost exclusively in cases where foreign partners were involved. Foreign firms, however, also often targeted dominant firms in CEE markets with the result that foreign ownership cemented rather than diluted market power.

Anti-competitive practices are even harder to prevent. Carlin et al. (1994) report that collusive behaviour is not uncommon among managers of firms in the same sector, a practice that was inherited from the socialist regime (Estrin and Cave, 1993). As Joskow et al. (1994) remind us, cross-firm collusion was often the only way to survive for firms and managers under the old regime, and established social norms of managerial conduct are not easy to break. OECD (1994b) reports such evidence from the Czech and Slovak Republics, suggesting that the authorities charged with enforcing competition policies were frequently unable to carry out their tasks properly in the face of deeply ingrained trade practices and the lack of independence from their national governments.

Trade Policies

According to Fingleton et al. (1996), trade regimes were initially liberalized substantially in the Visegrad countries. Restrictions were kept in place for 'sensitive products', but tariffs for most products were abolished. State monopolies for foreign transactions were swept away and non-tariff barriers to trade abolished. Messerlin (1995) notes that, in late 1990, Poland and the CSFR enjoyed the most liberal trade regimes in Europe, followed by Hungary, Romania and Bulgaria. Following the enthusiasm for free trade of the early transition years, however, the pendulum has swung back towards protectionism since the early 1990s (Csaba, 1995). New tariff restrictions were introduced following the first wave of imports from the EU in 1991–2. Basic tariffs were raised to 16% in Hungary, and 11% for industrial products and 18% for agricultural products in Poland. These average tariffs hide much higher tariffs for individual products. More significantly, there has been a growing tendency in the CEE countries to revert to non-tariff barriers to trade favouring exports of domestic industries, protecting domestic producers against foreign competition and creating special incentives for foreign investors (Messerlin, 1995; Csaba, 1995) and abusing trade policies for purposes of industrial policy (OECD 1994a, 1995). Csaba explains that this reversal reflects the growing effectiveness of special interest groups lobbying for protection. Lobbyism has increased as a result of the relatively high political volatility, reflected in frequent elections and government turnover, that increases the tendency of policy-makers to engage in short-sighted policies.

Messerlin argues that the Europe Agreements do not provide sufficient discipline for CEE trade policy to expect that these countries stick to the liberal policies ultimately required for accession to the EU. The Agreements contain only loose provisions regarding contingent protection and are only directed at CEE-EU trade. Both aspects make it unlikely that the Commission will expend much effort to enforce liberal trade regimes on the CEE countries on that basis. At the same time, he explains, the low legal status of trade laws in the CEE countries has exposed the trade regimes to political discretion. Finally, trade legislation passed in the late 1980s, even though it produced liberal rules, did not account sufficiently for the fact that individual trade barriers abolished by such laws can be easily substituted by other protectionist actions, such as tax laws targeting imports.

Csaba (1995), Messerlin (1995), and Winters (1995) all emphasize that the vulnerability of the new trade regimes to organized special interests demanding protectionism was facilitated by the lack of adequate institutional structures safeguarding liberal trade policies. Parliamentary procedures are too weak to limit the influence of legislators pursuing special interests of their constituencies. The lack of a strong ministry of trade overarching sectoral interests and imposing restraint on sectoral ministries implies that there is no strong advocate of liberal trade policies in the daily business of the government. The introduction of contingent protection implies a strong bias towards discretionary government intervention, in which the government regularly responds to groups seeking protection without facing countervailing opposition from groups supporting the general interest in limiting protection. These institutional weaknesses generate substantial uncertainty regarding the stability of the CEE countries' trade regimes and lead to the expectation that the tendency to revert to protectionism will, if anything, grow stronger over time.

This adverse expectation is also nourished by another observation in comments on the developments of EU-CEE trade. CEE policy-makers seem to be increasingly worried that trade between their countries and the EU has been skewed in favour of the EU in recent years. This has led to calls for policy adjustments to achieve a greater balance. Even economists have apparently failed to understand the fact that one cannot hope for both capital inflows into these countries as well as a balanced trade account. As in the United States in the 1980s, there is a substantial risk that the failure to recognize the link between net capital inflows and a current account deficit will ultimately fuel demands for more protectionism of domestic industries. Mounting economic nationalism and populist movements may exacerbate the importance of this confusion.

A review of these two central areas of Community economic policy shows that, despite the rapprochement of the CEE countries with the EU at a formal level of law-making, there are still many important open questions when it comes to the actual practice of economic policy. This leaves the Commission and the incumbent members of the EU with a large degree of uncertainty regarding the quality of economic policies in the CEE countries.

1.2.5 Constitutional Problems of the European Union

The current constitutional design of the European Union goes back to the original Treaty of Rome, the founding document of the European Community. It represents a careful compromise between two opposing political interpretations of European integration, the federalist one, which envisions a European federation as the ultimate goal, and the intergovernmental one, which regards European integration as a particular form of cooperation among sovereign nations. Since the former view supports the transfer of political sovereignty to the supranational EU and the latter view denies just that, a balance had to be found in defining how much sovereignty can be taken away from member states.

Three aspects of this compromise are particularly important in our current context. First, the decision-making bodies, originally designed for six members, have become increasingly unsuited to making timely and efficient decisions for a larger number of members. The eastward enlargement would dramatically increase this problem, as the number of members would increase to 22 or 25 states. Increasing the decision-making capability would require extending the domain of the majority rule in EU decisions, hence a further, dramatic shift of sovereignty to the Union. It would also require streamlining the Commission and the Council, hence less representation of individual states at the administrative centre of the Union. Finally, these reforms would increase the demand for democratic legitimacy of the Union's institutions through accountability to a politically stronger European Parliament. All these changes would meet fierce opposition from those who support the intergovernmental view of the EU.

The second constitutional aspect is that the Union, in the course time, has developed a true Union body of law going beyond intergovernmental agreements, the *acquis communautaire*. The *acquis* defines the common rights and obligations all members of the Union have under Union law. As a result of the struggle between the federalist and intergovernmental approaches to European integration, the *acquis* consists of a complicated set of rules, some of them fairly general, others very detailed; it lacks the hierarchy of laws ranging from constitutional to ordinary laws and ordinances typically found in national legal systems. Candidates for membership are presented the *acquis* as a rigid take-it-or-leave-it offer. The Union thus makes no room for flexible choices of the areas in which new members wish to participate.

The current debate over a reform of the EU's constitution has seen various proposals aimed at giving old and new members more flexibility in choosing the areas of cooperation (Dewatripont et al., 1995). The proposals have been welcomed by those countries that wish to extend European integration to new spheres of policy, e.g. France and Germany, and met the opposition of those who fear that more constitutional flexibility would result in first and second class membership, or lead to the deterioration of the Union into a network of loose intergovernmental cooperation arrangements.

The third constitutional aspect arises again from the conflict between the federalist and intergovernmental approaches. In the historical evolution of the EU, strong opposition against creating a powerful central EU administration has prevented the Union from developing its own mechanisms to enforce Union law. Following the German model of cooperative federalism instead, the Union relies on national administrations to implement Union law. Formally this is reflected in the fact that EU legislation must be translated into national law to become effective, and must be implemented and enforced by national administrations, and the absence of 'federal' police forces or a 'federal trade commission' as they exist in the United States. As a result, implementation of Union law, and particularly of Single Market legislation, varies across member states. Moreover, individual states may be slow in the translation of EU legislation into national law, and they may be lax or incompetent in its enforcement even after it has been translated. Dissatisfaction with the variation in quality of implementation of EU law has led to the call for strengthening the Union's own enforcement powers. In the US model of competitive federalism, where the federation has its own administrative functions, different enforcement capabilities of the member states matter much less, if at all. Creating such an administration, however, would again meet the opposition of all those who fear the weakening of the nation states relative to the European Union.

While a detailed discussion of these problems is beyond the scope of this paper (see Dewatripont et al., 1995 for an extensive survey and a proposal of *flexible integration*), the relevant point here is that a reform of the EU, to make it fitter for an eastward enlargement, necessary as it might be, will stir up delicate compromises among the incumbent members and will be resisted even by those who are not against enlargement *per se*.

1.3   Principles of the Political Economy of Accession

In this section we shed more light on the political economy of enlargement. We do so by developing a number of simple examples to highlight the relevant problems. Throughout the examples, we consider a hypothetical group of three countries, A, B, and C. Countries A and B, the incumbents, are already in an

Table 1 Country Pay-offs

Alternative	A	B	C
status quo	70	100	40
enlargement	80	115	50

economic union, and country C, the newcomer, has expressed its desire to join. Thus, countries A and B represent the current members of the EU, and C stands for the candidates for enlargement. Nothing substantial depends on the assumption of a single candidate; C might equally be interpreted as a group of countries wishing to join the union.

1.3.1 Positive Overall Benefits

We begin with the simplest and most obvious case in which the incorporation of the third country is beneficial to all parties. This case is represented by the pay-off matrix in Table 1.

We can think of these pay-offs as welfare-indices for each country, or, simplifying, levels of real income. The values of these pay-offs in the table are illustrative and not intended as estimates of actual welfare levels. In this interpretation, country B is a 'rich' member in the existing union, country A represents a middle-income country, while country C has a lower income than either one of the incumbents.

The table indicates that enlargement benefits all parties concerned and is therefore agreeable to all three countries. The fact that country B gains the largest benefit is not important for the conclusion that the incumbents should have no difficulty letting the newcomer in. This case represents the situation most economists would have in mind when thinking about the positive welfare effects of trade integration.

1.3.2 Distributional Problems

In practice, trade integration often leads to important distributional effects, i.e., the benefits from free trade among a group of countries is not as symmetric as suggested in the first example. Consider the following two situations illustrated in Table 2. In the first case, the benefits from integration are heavily skewed towards the incumbents because, for example, the newcomer's industries are less competitive than the incumbents' and therefore a period of restructuring is necessary to modernize the economy. Yet, enlargement is beneficial for the three countries taken as a group. The situation is reminiscent of EU enlargement involving Spain and Portugal. Countries A and B can share the surplus generated by enlargement through appropriate transfer mechanisms such as financing regional or structural adjustment projects in C's

Table 2   Pay-offs

Alternative	A	B	C
status quo	70	100	40
enlargement I	80	115	25
enlargement II	60	115	50

economy. This would reduce the pay-offs for A and B, but both could still gain enough to accept enlargement.

The second scenario in this table is the mirror image. In this case, the gains from enlargement are skewed towards countries B and C, but one of the incumbents loses out from enlargement. This might arise from the fact that the newcomer's factor endowments or industrial structure resemble closely that of country A but not that of country B. This illustrates the current fears among the southern European countries that the eastern enlargement would expose their relatively cheap labour-force to more price competition. Nevertheless, country A can be persuaded by country B promising to share the surplus through some appropriate transfer mechanism. Within the current context of the EU, this example suggests that the southern European member states would ask the northern states for compensation for their losses from enlargement by increasing the structural and regional funds paid to them.

If income transfers of the right kind can be made between the three countries, one should expect that enlargement will happen in both cases. This depends on two questions. The first one is whether transfers can be made without too much waste of resources. If so, the famous Coase theorem in economics says that enlargement will take place. In our context, the theorem says that the three countries will always settle on the efficient outcome—enlargement—regardless of the immediate distribution of the benefits from integration.[11]

In the European context, however, costless transfers cannot simply be assumed. The example of the CAP suggests that there can be substantial resource costs arising from transfer programmes, especially if such programmes are tied to particular uses and particular industries. As an illustration, suppose that for every pay-off unit transferred from one member to another, the union expends half a unit in transaction costs. In the first scenario, the incumbents would have to pay country C at least 15 units to make integration attractive to it. The cost of this transfer payment would reduce the total surplus by 7.5 units. As a result, A and B would be left with pay-offs of 68.75 and 103.75, respectively. This would obviously not be acceptable to country A which would oppose accession of the new member. In order to make country A indifferent, country B could compensate A with a similar transfer, keeping its pay-off at 70. But this in turn would reduce B's net pay-off to 101.9, so that the total surplus has almost completely vanished.

Thus, the efficiency of transfer programmes is essential for solving the distributional problems effectively. Economic analysis suggests that the efficient

Table 3 Country Pay-offs

Alternative	A	B	C
status quo, gross distribution	65	110	40
status quo, net distribution	70	100	40
enlargement, excluding C from transfers	75	115	45
enlargement, including C in transfers	67.5	107.5	55

solution would be to pay lump sum transfers without any links to sectoral or regional development criteria. Each country, however, would then have an incentive to understate its benefits from integration or to overstate its potential losses as a way to maximize its transfer receipts. Since the exact welfare pay-offs are hard to measure, the Union has an interest in tying transfer payments to variables which to some extent at least indicate welfare losses to avoid such moral hazard problems. The trade-off between measurability of the pay-offs and efficiency of the transfer system suggests that transaction costs will be relevant in the compensation of EU members for enlargement.

The second issue is that the incumbents may already have set up transfer schemes to solve earlier distribution problems. To illustrate this point, assume that the status quo in the preceding pay-off table reflects the working of a transfer scheme between A and B, with the gross and net pay-offs indicated in Table 3. For simplicity, we assume again that transfers can be made with no resource cost. The status quo required a transfer from B to A to make the original union viable. To sharpen the focus, we assume that enlargement benefits all parties, if C is excluded from the transfer scheme. If C participates in the scheme, however, country A turns from a net receiver to a net contributor, making its pay-off worse than without enlargement. This scenario illustrates the effects of German unification on fiscal equalization among German states as well as the current fears of the southern European states that enlargement would cost them their benefits from the existing regional and sectoral programmes of the EU.

In this example, the 'budgetary cost' of enlargement is represented by the increase in the volume of transfers paid within the enlarged community; an increase from five in the incumbent to ten in the enlarged union. In the scenario of Table 2, the 'budgetary cost' caused by enlargement consists of a transfer of 15 plus transactions costs of 7.5. Although current studies do not distinguish between these different types of budgetary costs, the point is important because the two scenarios call for different remedies. In the scenario of Table 2, the proper solution is to improve the efficiency of the transfer mechanism and then let C participate. In the scenario of Table 3, a possible solution is to exclude C from the pre-existing transfer scheme and aim at the gross distribution of pay-offs after enlargement; the various calls for graded membership of the CEE countries can be understood in this way. This is possible, because all three countries prefer this outcome over the status quo. Although country C prefers participation in the existing transfer scheme, it has no threat potential to force the others to accept that outcome. An alternative solution would be to rewrite the rules of the existing transfer scheme in such a way that A would remain a net receiver. As this may cause some groups in A to lose transfer benefits and may increase the payments some groups in B's society have to contribute, internal conflicts of distribution may make the adjustment politically very difficult. If so, the incumbents will ask country C to postpone participation in the transfer scheme until its income level is high enough to assure that A will not be a net contributor even under the old rules of the game.

1.3.3   Negative Externalities

So far, we have focused on scenarios where participation of the newcomer generates a surplus for the nascent group of three, although the distribution may be a problem. While this is the standard case of traditional trade theory, it need not always be true. Participation of a newcomer may generate negative spillovers on to the incumbent members of the integration group that make full participation of the additional country inefficient.

Financial market integration provides many examples of this. Trade in financial services such as insurance or banking services generates spillovers, since the stability of financial institutions depends largely on their reputation. Assume, for example, that banking markets were fully integrated, so that banks can take deposits anywhere in the integrated market regardless of where they are chartered. One important threat to the banking industry is the risk of contagious bank runs. Such a run occurs if the public, observing that an individual bank has become illiquid, believes this is a signal of liquidity problems in the banking sector in general. In such a situation, depositors may wish to withdraw their money immediately from other banks, too, since being the first in line is the best hedge against losing one's money. But if the run occurs, all banks become illiquid regardless of their financial situation before the first observation occurred. The lower the perceived financial soundness of the banking sector, the greater the likelihood of a run taking place. Deposit insurance and surrounding regulatory provisions and credible lender-of-last-resort functions can help prevent contagious runs, but regulation creates its own costs and inefficiencies. Thus, the better the perceived soundness of the banking sector, the less regulatory provisions are necessary and the more efficient the market outcome is. This means that including a country whose banking industry is not perceived, in the general public's view, as sufficiently

Table 4 Pay-offs

Alternative	A	B	C
status quo	70	100	40
narrow enlargement	90	120	50
broad enlargement	82	112	55

stable, in an integrated market for banking services, the need for additional regulation protecting banks in the other countries against contagious runs increases, and this lowers the pay-off from such integration to the countries with more developed banking markets.

To evaluate such a situation, consider the scenario of Table 4. Here, we distinguish between two economic sectors, say, goods markets and financial markets. According to the status quo, countries A and B have already achieved a common market in both sectors. Enlargement can proceed along two alternatives: a narrow enlargement, where C only participates in goods market integration, and a broad enlargement, where C participates in both fields of integration.

Table 4 illustrates the role of negative externalities. The important point is that including country C in the broader arrangement destroys part of the benefits financial market integration generates for countries A and B. The pay-off table suggests that the efficient way out is the narrow enlargement. Thus, the efficient response to negative externalities yields another justification for graded membership of the newcomer.

The current argument for excluding country C from some aspects of the integration arrangement is quite different from the ones discussed in the previous section. There, the restriction was a way to improve the distribution of the overall surplus to overcome the opposition of one incumbent. Here, the restriction is a way to generate additional surplus for all three countries. In the former case, the restriction could be avoided by revising the existing mechanism of redistribution within the old integration group, while in the current case, the final alternative is to wait until the source of the negative externality has disappeared in the course of economic development.

1.3.4 The Importance of Bundling and Compromise

The important argument against proposals for limited membership is that they ignore the importance of bundling political decisions as a means to reach compromise. Table 5 illustrates the problem. Here we consider the introduction of free trade between the incumbents and the newcomer in two hypothetical sectors or industries, X and Y. Free trade in X, say, manufactures, leads to overall welfare gains, but the gains are heavily skewed towards the incumbents. In the absence of transfer mechanisms, the newcomer will, therefore, oppose free entry of the incumbents' industries to his X-sector. The

Table 5   Pay-offs

Alternative	A	B	C
status quo	70	100	40
gains from free trade in sector X	15	20	−10
gains from free trade in sector Y	−5	−10	20
integration of both markets	80	110	50

situation is reversed in sector Y, say, food products. Here, the incumbents will oppose free trade, since their industries stand to lose from integration.

If the decisions regarding the two sectors are made separately, sectors X and Y will be excluded from integration. In contrast, if the decisions can be bundled, the newcomer and the incumbent can trade off losses in one sector against gains in the other and realize that free trade in both sectors simultaneously is welfare-increasing. Thus, it is important to structure enlargement negotiations in ways that allow political deals across narrow sectoral interests. This implies that the process of preparing the enlargement should not be left entirely to technocrats focusing narrowly on the specific problems of each sector. Political leadership is required to propose and accept deals, and this requires that the proper political decision-making institutions (the European Council in the EU) are involved (Smith et al., 1996).

Bundling decisions may be important for another reason. Each government negotiating in the enlargement process must at the same time secure sufficient domestic support for its policy. The problem here is that the internal distribution of the benefits from integration is not likely to be even. In particular, producers in protected markets in the incumbent union face the loss of monopoly rents, while producers in more competitive sectors expect an increase in producer surplus. In each case, consumers should expect an increase in consumer surpluses from increased competition. Practical experience with trade policy tells us that producer interests, because they are easier to organize, tend to prevail over consumer interests. This suggests that, when integration is considered separately in each sector, producers in the protected sector will succeed in preserving their position, i.e., this sector will not be included in the integration arrangement. Here, again, bundling is helpful, as it may enable the governments of the incumbent countries to mobilize enough support for free trade to overcome the opposition from producers in the protected sector. One way to do this is to present integration in all sectors as a take-it-or-leave-it package deal to the public.

In sum, proposals for limited integration are a double-edged sword. On the one hand, the limited integration approach can facilitate accession by mitigating the adverse effects of negative externalities and by avoiding the

Table 6   Pay-offs

Alternative	A	B	C
status quo	70	100	40
enlargement with good national implementation in C	80	110	50
enlargement with bad national implementation in C	60	90	60

need to redesign existing transfer schemes. On the other hand, this approach exposes the process of enlargement strongly to the influence of sectoral interests and this, in turn, can prevent efficient arrangements.

1.3.5   Uncertain Implementation of Union Law

As argued above, an important characteristic of the EU constitution is that the Union must rely heavily on national administrations to enforce Union law. In the context of enlargement, the uncertainty about the quality of implementation by the newcomers implies that the benefits from enlargement are uncertain. To illustrate the consequences, Table 6 contrasts two possible outcomes after enlargement. In the first case, the newcomer's degree of Union law implementation and enforcement is high and the surplus of integration is shared by it and the incumbents. In the alternative scenario, the newcomer is recalcitrant in implementing Union law, and the incumbents suffer welfare losses, because they have opened their markets to the newcomer and the latter exploits this access to its own advantage without any reciprocation. Ex ante, the incumbents do not know which case they will be in if they accept enlargement. Their assessment of the newcomer's credibility regarding proper implementation of Union law, is summarized in the probability α of being in the 'good' state. Clearly, if policy-makers in both countries are risk-neutral, enlargement is only acceptable if α is large enough to make the expected pay-offs at least as large as the status quo pay-offs, i.e., ≥ 0.5.[12]

Problems of this nature arise in the context of competition policy, where members may tolerate abusive market power, hidden state subsidies, or product standards and safety requirements with unduly lax national. They are also acute in the context of regulatory cooperation such as environmental policy (Dewatripont et al., 1995), where the gains come from prohibiting toxic emissions that pollute resources common to all three countries, or financial markets integration, where systemic stability is assured through banking and insurance regulation. The highest pay-offs here come from joint imposition of coordinated regulations. Such regulations, however, impose burdens on domestic industries. Country C might gain from not enforcing the common regulations, which gives its industries a competitive advantage, and free ride on the incumbents' efforts to reduce pollution or maintain financial stability. The incumbents would have to make even greater and more costly efforts to achieve the desired standards of environmental policy or financial market quality as a result.

What matters in these situations is the downside risk for the incumbents resulting from the possibility of adverse spillovers onto the incumbents or a skewed distribution of the benefits from integration when the common policies are improperly implemented in country C. The smaller the difference between the pay-offs in the status quo and in the 'bad' state, the greater the incumbents' willingness to accept the newcomer even with low credibility. If enlargement can be viewed as a process, this suggests that country C should participate first in areas with low downside risk for the incumbents. As time goes by and credibility is established (i.e., α grows bigger), the incumbents will be willing to extend country C's participation to areas with larger downside risks.

1.3.6   *Mutual Recognition vs. Harmonization*

As with every attempt at integration, the European Union has been torn between the principle that all members do the same (harmonization) and the principle that different members can reach the same goal in different ways (mutual recognition). Harmonization requires the Union to develop compromises between the relevant interests and cast them in detailed rules. Given the diversity of preferences among the member states in all areas of economic policy, such compromises may please no-one and agreement on harmonized policies is, therefore, often difficult. Mutual recognition can tolerate diversity to a much larger extent, but requires agreement on common rules of procedure and minimum standards to ensure that the common goal is effectively met.

Since the mid-1980s, the 'new' approach to regulatory policy emphasizing mutual recognition has become the dominant strategy of dealing with product regulation and standardization in the EU. In fact, switching to the new approach has revived the Union's ability to act in these matters, an important step in the development of the Single Market. This reflects a strong preference of the incumbent member states for regulatory diversity aimed at common regulatory goals.

Since mutual recognition decentralizes economic policies, it requires trust that all parties behave according to the agreed rules. Therefore, the main problem with mutual recognition is uncertainty about any member's ability or willingness to abide by the rules. Here, again, the EU's lack of its own enforcement powers adds to the problem. Enlargement with new countries whose credibility in this regard is still weak may, therefore, shift the balance back towards harmonization and endanger the benefits of the Single Market reaped under the 'new' approach.

Table 7   Pay-offs

Alternative	A	B	C
status quo	70	100	40
harmonization with good implementation	75	105	45
harmonization with bad implementation	74	104	50
mutual recognition with good implementation	80	110	55
mutual recognition with bad implementation	71	101	60

Consider the example of Table 7. Here, we assume that once enlargement has happened, two regulatory approaches can be taken in the further development of the Single Market, one in which harmonization dominates and one in which mutual recognition dominates. To sharpen the focus, we assume that the expected pay-off from enlargement is positive under both options. Given the revealed preference of the incumbents for mutual recognition, we assume that their pay-offs in the 'good' state, when the newcomer implements common policies properly, are larger under mutual recognition than under harmonization. Harmonization, however, gives the Union more control over the material content of regulatory provisions in the new member state, reducing the risk of lax enforcement. This suggests that the downside risk for the incumbents is lower under harmonization. In the table, this is reflected in the fact that the differences in pay-off between the 'good' and the 'bad' state are smaller under harmonization than under mutual recognition.

The credibility of the newcomer now influences the incumbents' between regulatory regimes. If the credibility of the newcomer is sufficiently low ($\alpha < 0.58$), the incumbents will prefer harmonization, although harmonization promises substantially lower benefits than mutual recognition if the newcomer implements the common policies properly. The greater the downside risk under mutual recognition, the larger the preference for harmonization will be. The corollary is that countries with a strong preference for regulatory diversity will oppose enlargement if it creates a bias towards harmonization.

1.3.7   Whither the Median Voter?

Enlargement implies not only access of the newcomers to the incumbents' markets but also their participation in the common decision-making mechanisms. The current debate over enlargement has taken issue with this aspect mostly from the point of view of decision-making rules in the European

Figure 1

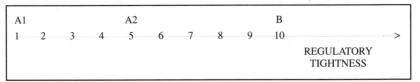

Council and the size of the European Commission and proposed different ways of redesigning the Union's decision making-rules.[13] Here, we wish to stress another aspect of enlargement. Current arrangements in the EU reflect the balance of many competing interests between the member states and sometimes even within the member states, viz. the conflict between consumers and producers, especially agricultural producers. Bringing in new members threatens to upset this balance depending on the newcomers' preferences relative to the incumbents' preferences as reflected in the current compromises. If the newcomers' preferences were known with certainty, the incumbents could preserve their inherited compromises by properly allocating votes in the common decision-making institutions. Yet, again, uncertainty changes the picture.

To illustrate, we assume in Figure 1 that there are three incumbent members, A1, A2, and B, and two newcomers, C1 and C2. Consider the choice of a regulatory regime for the Union as an example. To simplify, we assume that regulatory regimes can be ranked according regulatory tightness on a scale from one to ten, one describing a loose, hands-off regime and ten a tight, interventionist regime. Among the incumbents, preferences are such that A1 prefers a loose regime (1), A2 an intermediate regime (5), and B an interventionist regime (10). Let the inherited voting rules give A1 and A2 two votes each in common decisions, while B has three votes. For the sake of simplicity, we let all decisions be made my simple majority; nothing substantial hinges on this point in our context. Then, the regulatory regime adopted by the incumbents is an intermediate one, since A2 is the pivotal voter.

Consider now the issue of enlargement and assume that C1 and C2 can be of two types. Each may either prefer a relatively loose regime (1.5) or a moderately tight regime (7.5). Before the enlargement, the incumbents can design new voting rules, and these, together with enlargement, must be adopted with unanimity.

If the newcomers' preferences were known with certainty, the solution would be straightforward. The incumbents would choose voting rules such that the inherited compromise would not be changed. Specifically, if one of the newcomers is of the loose type and the other one of the moderately tight one, any number of votes evenly given to both would preserve the old balance and be agreeable to the incumbents. If both were of the loose type, the incumbents would increase their votes by one for A1 and A2 and two for B and give C1 and C2 one vote each, which leaves A2 as the pivotal voter. If both were of the moderately tight type, in contrast, A1 and A2 would demand even more votes, at least four each, if B obtains five and C1 and C2 one each. Although this might look like shifting the balance of power towards A1 and A2, it would be agreeable for C.

The situation is different when the incumbents do not know the regulatory preferences of the newcomers. In that case, votes cannot be allocated in the way described above. Instead, they have to be allocated according to some observable variable, such as country size. Thus, assume that for each newcomer the probability of being of either type is one half. If the newcomers both obtain one vote (because they are of smaller size than A1 and A2), the expected regulatory regime is tighter, since the expected value on the scale is 5.63. In contrast, if both newcomers obtain two votes (because they are the same size as A1 and A2), the expected regulatory regime is looser, with an index of 4.75. But this implies that neither outcome will be agreeable to all three incumbents. Thus, enlargement will not be accepted with unanimity.

1.4   Strategies for Enlargement for the CEE Countries

To summarize section 1.3, there are two types of difficulties with the eastern enlargement. On the one hand, there are the problems connected with achieving a proper distribution of the benefits from integration and avoiding negative externalities. On the other hand, there is the uncertainty problem regarding the newcomers' implementation of Union law and their future policy preferences. In thinking about enlargement strategies for the CEE countries it is important to keep these two types of difficulties apart, since they call for different responses in the design of the enlargement process.

1.4.1   Overcoming Distributional Problems

The discussion in section 1.3 indicates that the solution of the distributional and negative externality problems is, in principle, fairly straightforward. The main requirement is that the CEE countries renounce participation in existing transfer mechanisms and some parts of European integration at least temporarily in exchange for obtaining mechanisms specifically designed for this enlargement and that these be designed efficiently enough to avoid a waste of resources. An important consideration here is that the CEE countries constitute a group of large economic heterogeneities. From the distributional aspect, this suggests that each individual member of this group will cause and face its own, specific problems with enlargement. For example, distributional problems connected to the CAP will be much smaller in the context of the accession of the Czech Republic or Slovenia than in the context of Romania's or even Hungary's accession. Similarly, Hungary and the Czech Republic can be expected to have reasonably stable financial markets much earlier than other states in the region, implying that negative externalities arising from financial sector instability would be much less of a problem in these countries.

The implication is that any attempt to design a uniform enlargement strategy treating all CEE countries in the same way will (rightfully) lead to disenchantment among the less problematic cases, the countries that will feel their accession is being held back because of the more problematic candidates. Strategies focusing on overcoming the distributional problems, therefore, have little room for developing a joint accession strategy or even regional cooperation. This suggests that the way to proceed is to develop country-specific strategies on the basis of the individual Europe Agreements.

This leaves it up to each individual CEE country to tackle accession on its own. Nevertheless, all countries will face choices along the same lines. A proper balance must be found between limiting the degree of EU membership to reduce the size of the distributional problems on the one hand, and deterioration of the accession process into cherry-picking only those elements of EU membership that are most convenient for the individual country on the other.

A related strategic requirement is that the importance of sectoral negotiations must not become too large, as sectoral interest groups would become too influential otherwise. Political leadership must be involved in the process. Since this cannot be delivered steadily over long time periods, agreement on as many details as possible of the enlargement process should be reached quickly.

To facilitate speedy accession, the CEE countries should, under this approach, strive to assimilate the EU's legal framework into their legal systems as much as possible. Technical assistance from the Union can be expected for this, so that the resource costs should be manageable. As adoption of legal texts similar to EU texts has already largely been achieved, the CEE countries should now focus on the next step: the translation of laws into administrative directives and procedures.

1.4.2 The Option Value of Waiting for Enlargement

The uncertainty surrounding enlargement creates much bigger problems. From the perspective of the incumbents, enlargement has the following characteristics: (1) it is irreversible, since the EU has no exit procedure; (2) it involves a large transfer of property rights (the rights of being a member) to the newcomers which, in view of the first point, is a sunk cost once it has happened; (3) the expected benefits are low initially but grow over time, since the sources of negative externalities go away, the newcomers' incomes move closer to the incumbents' incomes, and uncertainty about the newcomers' ability and willingness to implement common policies, as well as their policy preferences, is gradually reduced. These three characteristics are typical for problems which generate an *option value of waiting*: postponing enlargement involves only a small cost for the incumbents since the expected benefits foregone are low. Postponement means that the fixed investment is not incurred immediately, part of the uncertainty is resolved, and the expected benefits are allowed to increase. From the incumbents' point of view, therefore, it is optimal to wait until the expected benefits from enlargement have grown sufficiently to outweigh the fixed investment.

This structure is clearly visible in the EU's current approach towards the CEE countries. In contrast to earlier enlargements, the association agreements with the CEE countries do not contain an explicit perspective for enlargement. A target date has not been set, nor has a specific catalogue of entry requirements been drawn up. The EU's acknowledgement of the CEE countries' interest in joining came with the explanation that enlargement would have to be postponed until the candidates were ready to fulfil the duties of full membership, but also until the EU was ready to take them in as new members. Avoiding all commitments regarding the timing of enlargement maximizes the option value of waiting.

The essential requirement of an enlargement strategy from this perspective is to reduce the option value of waiting as much and as fast as possible. Key elements are reducing the EU's initial investment and the uncertainty connected with the enlargement.

Limiting the EU's Initial Investment

Limiting the size of the initial investment requires limiting the scope of the property rights granted to the new members. With regard to EU-CEE trade this can be achieved by combining the general and complete abolition of all existing tariffs and quantitative trade barriers with the provision that the EU could impose trade barriers aimed at quality standards and product safety. Thus, instead of applying the principle of mutual recognition in such standards, CEE products would have to be certified by the national bodies of at least one incumbent EU member state to obtain access to EU markets.

A similar procedure cannot be applied in the enforcement of competition law and trade law. Here, the EU could retain the right to impose contingent protection measures aimed at neutralizing the distorting effects cartels, dominant firms or government subsidies have on CEE product prices. Note that this is different from conditional protectionism currently included in the Europe Agreements, the conditionality of which is tied to crisis situations in the EU markets. From the point of view of the uncertainty problem, the role of such measures would be to have a flexible response to uncompetitive behaviour rather than distributional conflicts.

Problems with standards in the environment, safety in the workplace and traffic regulation could, in principle, be dealt with in the same way. Again, the EU would grant the CEE countries market access assuming proper implementation of environmental standards. Where such implementation is lacking, the EU would then impose a temporary tariff offsetting the cost-differential resulting from the use of less environmentally friendly production processes. Note that this is in line with economic efficiency. It is often argued that the demand for a clean environment has an income elasticity greater than one, i.e., it grows more than proportionally with rising standards of living. This implies that countries with low incomes should be allowed to live with lower environmental standards than high-income countries. Equivalently, it is argued that imposing high standards on the CEE countries would result in excessive costs dedicated to environmental purposes from the CEE perspective.[14]

The procedure outlined here takes this into account. CEE countries that wish to postpone ambitious environmental policies can do so. They would not, however, be able to use the resulting competitive advantage in trade with the EU. In economic terms, the offsetting tariff would correct the distortion resulting from low-priced environmental resources in trade with the EC, but the CEE countries would still not be forced to spend resources they prefer to invest elsewhere on environmental policies whose effects would be felt not only by local producers but also by local consumers.

While these measures, at a first glance, appear not too different from the graded-membership approach discussed above, they actually are. The focus here is not on excluding sectors that create distributional problems, but on giving the EU the possibility to offset market distortions that result from the specific conditions prevailing in the transition economies when there is sufficient reason to assume non-compliance with EU product standards or rules of competition. For the transition phase, such measures would replace reliable enforcement at the national level, until this can be delivered by national authorities. We emphasize that the measures discussed here should not take a sectoral approach per se or be understood as excluding entire sectors from the enlargement process, as this would give distributional interests inappropriately large weight in the decision-making process. Instead, offsetting tariffs would apply to specific products and producers.

An important question is, who should have the authority to impose contingent trade barriers of this kind? Technically, the European Commission could play that role.[15] A number of reasons speak against that solution, however. First, to be accepted as a fair procedure, the CEE countries should have a voice in it. Second, the Commission would then deal with the specific trade relations with the CEE countries in the broader context of EU policies. This would create a bias in favour of using EU laws as standards, where the idea is to give the CEE countries room for deviating from EU legislation in the process of accession. Third, the sectoral institutional organization of the Commission would make these decisions prone to be captured by sectoral special interests within the EU, i.e., they would deteriorate into protectionist trade barriers to shelter non-competitive industries in the EU.

A preferred solution would be to set up a new institution, the Accession Council, an independent authority charged with supervising EU-CEE trade relations during the transition phase. The Accession Council would have the right to impose contingent trade barriers as discussed above. It would receive complaints from EU consumers and producers and hear the Commission and the CEE administrations and producers concerned. This authority would also receive the reports from national certification organizations regarding compliance of CEE products with EC standards and issue the product certification. The Accession Council would be composed of individuals with the proper expertise from the EU and the CEE countries. To strengthen its independent position, a single Accession Council should be responsible for EU relations with all CEE countries. Former GATT (General Agreement on Tariffs and Trade) and now WTO (World Trade Organization) anti-dumping procedures and the methods for conflict resolution between the EU and the European Free Trade Association in the European Economic Area agreement provide examples for the design of the Accession Council.

Building Credibility

At the heart of the informational uncertainty problem lies the fact that the countries emerging from socialist regimes have had no or little chance to prove their commitment to market-oriented policies compatible with open and competitive markets as required by the Treaty on European Union. The literature dealing with credibility issues suggests that there are two main ways to gain credibility. One is the creation of appropriate institutions.[16] The other is to establish a track record of consistent policies: the more often a government resists the temptation to give in to short-term or particular interests, the more its foreign counterparts or the Commission will see the continuation of such behaviour as likely.

The Commission's White Paper emphasizes the importance of building an institutional structure lending credibility to the willingness and ability of the CEE's national governments to implement properly Single Market policies. Since the lack of credibility in this area is a common problem to all CEE countries, an initial strategy for accession could be for these countries to build appropriate institutions jointly rather than separately. Specifically, instead of creating separate, national administrations charged with the implementation of the Single Market, groups of CEE countries could set up joint institutions with that mission, such as a joint competition authority, a joint environmental agency, a joint standardization board, and joint authorities charged with the regulation of financial markets. An obvious way to start this would be a joint institutional framework in the Visegrad group.

CEE cooperation in this area would have a number of significant advantages. First, economies of scale could be realized by pooling administrative functions and resources. This is particularly important in the CEE countries given that new administrative functions fit for market economies must be created in many parts of the economies. Second, the partner countries in such cooperations could benefit from each others' experience in the implementation of market-oriented procedures and policies. Third, cooperation in this way would build a track record for the participants in international cooperation. This would become an important signal for the EU that CEE commitment to international cooperation is credible: the counterargument, that CEE governments find cooperation with other governments in the region politically unattractive obviously serves to arouse suspicion in the Union that these governments will not behave cooperatively as members of the EU.¨

Finally, negotiations with the EU during the accession phase would be centralized in such a way that the Commission would talk to the joint authority of groups of CEE countries instead of to several national authorities simultaneously. This would increase the bargaining power of the CEE countries and create more room for deviation of national policies from EU policies in the accession phase, which, as discussed earlier, is desirable in view of the very specific problems related to transformation.

It is in this regard that the idea of a regional integration scheme among the CEE countries preceding accession to the EU gains relevance. Rather than focusing on free trade—the Central European Free Trade Area (CEFTA) is limited in scope particularly in the transition phase, when old industry structures still determine CEE production patterns—such a regional integration scheme should focus on joint institution building. Another, significant advantage of such integration could be realized if it included integrated regulatory regimes for financial markets. For the CEE countries, the fact that regulatory regimes for financial institutions are still only emerging at the national level suggests that the choice between harmonization versus mutual recognition should not be a very difficult one at this point. Harmonizing regulatory regimes could, however, allow these economies to reap economies of scale in such markets and yet achieve a regulatory regime that meets the specific needs of the transition phase.

Building a track record showing that the governments are truly committed to competitive market economies is the other important element of gaining credibility. The most important problem here is *time-inconsistency*. Time-inconsistency describes the phenomenon that it is often in the best perceived interest of a government to renege on previously announced policies.¨ Regulatory policies provide ample examples of this. Consider a government announcing that banks extending more than, say, 30% of their portfolio in loans to a single customer will not have access to the government's lending-of-last-resort function. *Ex ante*, this is a sensible announcement since the government wants to reduce its own and the taxpayers' exposure to the risk of paying for bad bank loans. Suppose that a large bank actually lends more than 30% of its portfolio to a customer who then goes under. leaving the bank illiquid and with no capital. The government then faces the choice between letting the bank go under and allowing depositors to lose their money and other companies to lose their credit relations, or breaking its promise and bailing out the bank. Since the financial damage from the large customer's bankruptcy has already occurred, and the additional financial damage from closing down the bank could easily be larger than a bailout, a short-sighted government will likely find a bailout more attractive than a bank failure. But once the public realizes that the government is indeed short-sighted, more and more breaches of the regulatory rule will occur as people anticipate that the government will step in, if loans turn bad. Thus, more and more bailouts will take place over time. It takes a more far-sighted government to realize the cost of lost credibility that such a bailout entails.

Building a track record is important, then, because it establishes the government's reputation as being far-sighted. In our context, two aspects deserve particular attention. First, building credibility does not require a track record immediately in all fields of economic policy. From this perspective, an accession strategy can be focused on individual sectors, where implementation of market-oriented policies is completed relatively fast, while the stage of implementation in other sectors is still much lower. Given the scarcity of administrative resources in the CEE countries, focusing on individual sectors can be important to speed up the process of accession. The design of an accession strategy then requires identifying which sectors should be addressed first and which later. Obviously, regional integration along the lines discussed above would be helpful to make sure that a focused strategy does not become overly narrow.

Second, to reduce the time-inconsistency problem, it is important that policies oriented towards the long run promise reasonable benefits in the foreseeable future from the government's point of view. This means that CEE governments should aim for policies that are optimal given the specific needs of a transition economy. As discussed above, this can and will often mean different policies from current EU legislation. Thus, building a track record for credible commitment to market-oriented policies can involve significant differences from EU legislation for some time during the accession phase. By making it harder to overcome the time-inconsistency problem, rapid approximation of CEE legislation to EU law can obstruct rather than facilitate timely accession. Although it may seem contradictory to implement policies in the CEE countries that first deviate from EU policies, the positive credibility effect will eventually make accession easier.

1.5   Conclusion

The debate over the eastern enlargement of the EU has until now focused mainly on the distributional difficulties generated by membership of countries in transition and with low income levels. In this paper, we have argued that the enlargement problem has another dimension. Uncertainty about the potential new members and the quality of their economic policies creates an option value of postponing enlargement. The distributional problems seen in isolation suggest that the design of an enlargement that generates an acceptable distribution of pay-offs for all countries involved is possible. The key is to limit the candidate countries' participation in those areas of the EU that generate the largest distributional problems. Solutions to the uncertainty problem resemble these in that they limit the initial investment of property rights by the Union. They also, however, call for institution building and a gradual rather than rapid approximation of the CEE's legal systems to those of the EU.

Perhaps the greatest difficulty with a mutual agreement of the terms of accession is that CEE governments might mistake the Union's concerns caused by the uncertainty problem for disguised attempts to postpone enlargement to avoid solutions to the distributional questions. Naturally, the CEE countries put less weight on the uncertainty problem than the incumbent EU. Nevertheless, a timely enlargement requires that both sides recognize the problem and develop appropriate strategies to overcome it.

Notes

* This paper was prepared for the Economic Policy Initiative of the Centre for Economic Policy Research and the Institute for EastWest Studies. I thank my discussants, Jenö Koltai, Laszlo Csaba, Graham Mahew, and Joan Pearce for their helpful comments and the participants of the EPI forum for insightful comments.

1. See Swann (1992) for a discussion.
2. Der Spiegel 42, 1991, p. 24, quoted from Pinder (1994).
3. See Trade Liberalization With Central and Eastern Europe, *European Economy* Suppl. A 7, 1994.
4. See *European Economy* Suppl. A 7, 1994.
5. Some observers have complained that the new trade administrations in the CEE countries are being taught to operate in an environment of managed trade rather than free trade, and fear that this might bias CEE policies too much towards government intervention.
6. In some sensitive sectors, the impact may even by positive, as the outsourcing of some labour-intensive activities to CEE countries such as textiles, may help EU workers in the remaining activities to survive competition against third competitors in Asia and elsewhere (Corado, 1995).
7. Tangermann (1993) estimates that a full use of these quotas would allow Poland and Hungary to ship about 4% of their potential agricultural exports to the EU.
8. The aggressive wage policies West German unions managed to push through in East Germany regardless of their consequences in terms of job destruction and fiscal transfers to East Germany testifies clearly for this (von Hagen, 1995).
9. See e.g., von Hagen and Walz (1995) for a model highlighting the importance of expectations for migration flows.
10. See the country studies in Weidenfeld (1995).

11. See Dewatripont et al. (1995) for a similar argument.
12. If policy-makers are risk-averse, which is more plausible in reality, even greater credibility will be required to accept enlargement.
13. Proposals for reform include abolishing the current rule of one or two commissioners for each member state and the rotation presidencies of the European Council. See Dewatripont et al. (1995).
14. Note that the issue here must be kept separate from the EU's own interest in environmental protection in the CEE countries. Nuclear energy is the most drastic example: all EU states have an obvious interest in high safety standards for nuclear power plants in the East. Other examples of environmental spillovers are easily found. This, however, is a different problem from the trade distortions described above. Under the setup outlined above, nothing would prevent the EU from subsidizing environmental protection in the CEE countries because the EU itself would benefit from their results. Trade policy should not be involved in such decisions.
15. The European Court cannot play such a role because legal proceedings are generally not fast enough.
16. The most prominent examples in economics are the independence of central banks and of the courts. In both cases, taking important decisions out of the hands of the government and entrusting them to an institution not driven by short-term political interests serve as a means to avoid the adverse effects of lacking credibility: persistent inflation in the first case and weak property rights in the second.
17. See the statement of Commissioner van den Broek (1996) at the opening of the EPI forum.
18. See Kydland and Prescott for a classic exposition of the problem.

References

Baldwin, R., Begg, D., Danthine, J. P., Grilli, V., Haaland, J., Neumann, M. J. M., Norman, V., Venables, A. and Winters, A. (1992): *Is Bigger Better? The Economics of EC Enlargement*, Monitoring European Integration 3, London, Centre for Economic Policy Research.

Baldwin, R. E. (1993): 'The Potential for Trade Between the Countries of EFTA and Central and East Europe', Occasional Paper No. 44, EFTA, Economic Affairs Department, Geneva.

Baldwin, R. E. (1994): *Towards an Integrated Europe*, London, Centre for Economic Policy Research.

Bofinger, P. (1995): 'The Political Economy of the Eastern Enlargement of the EU', CEPR Discussion Paper 1234, London.

Brunner, P. and Ochel, W. (1995): 'Die Europäische Union zwischen Vertiefung und Erweiterung', *ifo schnelldienst* 32, 16 November 1995, pp. 9–20.

Carlin, W., van Reenen, J. and Wolfe, T. (1994): 'Enterprise Restructuring in the Transition: An Analytical Survey of the Case Study Evidence from Central and Eastern Europe', EBRD Working Paper 14, London.

Cave, M. and Estrin, S. (1994): 'Introduction', in S. Estrin and M. Cave (eds.), *Competition and Competition Policy*, London, Pinter.

Corado, C. (1995): 'The Textiles and Clothing Trade with Central and Eastern Europe: Impact on Members of the EC', in R. Faini and R. Portes (eds.), *European Union Trade with Eastern Europe*, London, Centre for Economic Policy Research, pp. 236–68.

Coricelli, F. (1996): 'Fiscal Constraints, Reform Strategies, and the Speed of Transition: The Case of Central and Eastern Europe', CEPR Discussion Paper 1339, London.

Csaba, L. (1995): 'The Political Economy of Trade Regimes in Central Europe', in L. A. Winters (ed.), *Foundations of an Open Economy*, London, Centre for Economic Policy Research.

De Benedictis, L. and Padoan, P. C. (1994): 'EC Enlargement to Eastern Europe: Community and National Incentives and Sectoral Resistances', in S. Lombardini and P. C. Padoan (eds.), *Europe Between East and South*, Dordrecht, Kluwer.

Dewatripont, M., Giavazzi, F., von Hagen, J., Harden, I., Persson, T., Roland, G., Rosenthal, H., Sapir, A. and Tabellini, G. (1995): *Flexible Integration*, Monitoring European Integration 6, London, Centre for Economic Policy Research.

Drabek, Z. (1994): 'A Call for Renegotiations of the Europe Agreement', *Prague Economic Papers* 2, pp. 135–50.

Estrin, S. and Cave, M. (1993): *Competition and Competition Policy: A Comparative Analysis of Central and Eastern Europe*, London, Pinter.

European Commission (1995): *Vorbereitung der Assoziierten Staaten Mittel- und Osteuropas auf die Integration in den Binnenmarkt der Union*, Weißbuch KOM(95) 163 endg., Brussels, (White Paper on the preparation of the associated countries of central and eastern Europe for integration into the internal market of the EU.)

European Commission, Directorate General II (1994): 'The Economic Interpenetration Between the European Union and Eastern Europe', *European Economy* 6, reports and studies, Brussels.

Faini, R. and Portes, R. (1995): 'Opportunities Outweigh Adjustment: The Political Economy of Trade with Central and Eastern Europe', in R. Faini and R. Portes (eds.), *European Union Trade with Eastern Europe*, London, Centre for Economic Policy Research, pp. 1–18.

Feinberg, R. M. and Meurs, M. (1994): 'Privatization and Antitrust in Eastern Europe: The Importance of Entry', *Antitrust Bulletin*, Fall, pp. 797–811.

Fingleton, J., Fox, E., Neven, D. and Seabright, P. (1996): *Competition Policy and the Transformation of Central Europe*, London, Centre for Economic Policy Research.

Foralczyk, A. (1994): 'Competition Policy in the Polish Economy in Transition', in M. Cave and S. Estrin (1994).

Gabrisch, H. (1995): *Die Integration der mittel- und osteuropäischen Länder in die europäische Wirtschaft*, Institut für Wirtschaftsforschung Halle, Sonderheft 1–95.

Gasiorek, M., Smith, A. and Venables, A. (1994): 'Modelling the Effect of Central and East European Trade on the European Community', in DGII, European Commission (1994), pp. 519–38.

Grosfeld, I. and Roland, G. (1995): 'Defensive and Strategic Restructuring in Central European Enterprises', CEPR Discussion Paper 1135, London.

Guggenbhhl, A. (1995): 'The Political Economy of Association with Eastern Europe', in F. Laursen (ed.), *The Political Economy of European Integration*, Dordrecht, Kluwer.

Heinemann, F. (1995): 'EU-Osterweiterung und Kohäsionspolitik', Discussion Paper 95–01, Zentrum für Europäische Wirtschaftspolitik.

Hoffmann, L. (1994): 'Problems and Perspectives of East-West Economic Relations', in S. Lombardini and P. C. Padoan (eds.), *Europe Between East and South*, Dordrecht, Kluwer.

Joskow, P. L., Schmalensee, R. and Tsukanova, N. (1994): 'Competition Policy During and After Transition in Russia', *Brookings Papers on Economic Activity: Microeconomics*, pp. 301–81.

Kawecka-Wyrzykowska, E. (1996): 'Cost and Benefits of the Eastward Enlargement of the EU: Selected Issues', draft, Foreign Trade Institute, Warsaw.

Koop, M. J. and Nunnenkamp, P. (1994): 'Die Transformationskrise in Mittel- und Osteuropa: Ursachen und Auswege', *Die Weltwirtschaft*, pp. 67–92.

Kuschel, H. D. (1995): 'Das Europaabkommen der EG mit Polen', Bundesministerium für Wirtschaft, Sys05/PL.

Messerlin, P. A. (1995): 'CEEs' Trade Laws in the Light of International Experience', in L. A. Winters (ed.), *Foundations of an Open Economy*, London, Centre for Economic Policy Research.

Orlowski, L. (1995): 'Preparations of the Visegrad Countries for Admission to the EU: Monetary Policy Aspects', *Economics of Transition* 3, pp. 333–353.

Pinder, J. (1994): 'Conditions of Enlargement to Central Europe: Social Market Economy, Pluralist and Federal Democracy', in J. Redmond (ed.), *Prospective Europeans*, New York, Harvester Wheatsheaf.

Rollo, J. and Smith, A. (1993): 'The Political Economy of Eastern European Trade with the EC: Why So Sensitive', Economic Policy 16, pp. 140–181.

Rosati, D. (1995): 'Impediments to Poland's Accession to the European Union: Real or Imaginary?', in E. Kawecka-Wyrzykowska and T. Roe (eds.), *Polish Agriculture and Enlargement of the European Union*, Warsaw School of Economics.

Sabi, M. (1996): 'Comparative Analysis of Foreign and Domestic Bank Operations in Hungary'. *Journal of Comparative Economics* 22, pp. 179–88.

Slay, B. (1995): 'Industrial Demonopolization and Competition Policy in Poland and Hungary'. *Economics of Transition* 3, pp. 479–504.

Smith, A., Holmes, P., Sedelmeier, U., Smith, E., Wallace, H. and Young, A. (1996): *The European Union and Central and Eastern Europe: Pre-Accession Strategies*, Sussex European Institute Paper 15, Sussex.

Tangermann, S. (1993): 'Some Economic Effects of EC Agricultural Trade Preferences for Central Europe', *Journal of Economic Integration* 8, pp. 152–74.

Thiel, M. (1995): 'Das Wettbewerbs- und Kartellrecht in Osteuropa', *Osteuropa-Recht*, pp. 99–120.

Tirole, J. (1994): 'Western Prudential Regulation: Assessment and Reflections on its Application to Central and Eastern Europe', *Economics of Transition* 2, pp. 129–150.

Van den Broek, H. (1996): 'The Challenge of Enlargement for the Candidate Countries', Institute for EastWest Studies, mimeo (Brussels, 7 June).

Von Hagen, J. (1995): 'East Germany: The Economics of Kinship', CEPR Discussion Paper 1296, London.

Von Hagen, J. and Walz, U. (1995): 'Social Security and Migration in an Ageing Europe', in B. Eichengreen, J. Frieden and J. von Hagen (eds.), *Politics and Institutions in an Integrated Europe*, Heidelberg and New York, Springer Verlag.

Weidenfeld, W., ed. (1995): *Mittel- und Osteuropa auf dem Weg in die Europäische Union*, Gütersloh, Bertelsmann Verlag.

Welfens, P. J. J. (1995): 'Die Europäische Union und die mitteleuropäischen Länder. Entwicklungen, Probleme, politische Optionen', Bericht des Bundesinstituts für ostwissenschaftliche und internationale Studien, Köln.

Whitley, R. (1995): 'Transformation and Change in Europe: Critical Themes', in E. J. Dittrich, G. Schmidt and R. Whitley (eds.), *Industrial Transformation in Europe*, London, Sage.

Witkowska, J. (1994): 'Functioning of the Market Economy in Poland. Barriers to Closer Integration into the EU', *Osteuropa Wirtschaft* 39, pp. 128–34.

World Trade Organisation (1995): *Regionalism and the World Trading System*, Geneva.

Wysokinska, Z. (1994): 'Assoziierungsabkommen zwischen Polen und der EG— Richtungen der Liberalisierung der Handelsumsätze", *Osteuropa Wirtschaft* 39, pp. 55–70.

2

The CEE Countries' Aspirations for Enlargement

Andrej Kumar
University of Ljubljana

2.1   Introduction

The aspirations and policies for incorporating the countries of Central and Eastern Europe (CEE) into the European Union (EU) are determined by two sets of conditions. The first set is related to the economic, geographic, political, cultural and historical specificities of CEE. The second set of conditions is defined by the interests and attitudes of the present members of the EU as they relate to the decisions it needs to make in order to 'deepen' and 'enlarge' the integration.

It is obviously not necessary that both sets of conditions in general would converge towards the same ultimate goal, which could be defined as granting full membership of the CEE countries in the EU in the near future. Below, I will concentrate on describing the position of CEE and the level of its economic development, and the countries' aspirations concerning their future full membership. Due to the uncertainties surrounding the future extent of internal integration within the EU, and in addition, due to the not yet entirely clear attitude of the EU to further instances of enlargement, I will not focus on attempts to estimate a probable (or wished) future moment in time when the EU would grant membership to some of the CEE countries. In my understanding the enlargement of the EU is a process, the successful realization of which is in the interest of both the present EU members and the CEE countries.

2.2   Preliminaries on the CEE Countries

Each country in the CEE group is in the middle of the process of transition towards fully fledged market economies and also faces the task of constructing democratic political institutions. But one has to recognise a manifold diversity among these nations. The viewpoints of geography, history, culture and politics all compel us to look at each country individually—from the Baltics in the North to the Balkans in the South.

The members of the CEE group could be reasonably divided into two major subgroups. The first of these contains those counties which have already concluded their European Association Agreements (EAA) with the EU. Since June 1996 this group consists of ten countries. The second comprises the countries which are related to the Commonwealth of Independent States (CIS). It is customary to include 19 countries in CEE (see Eurobarometer, pp. 6–7). However, the definition just offered could produce some inaccuracies.

Slovenia, for example, has not been a country with an EAA (until June 1996), and has not been a CIS country either. The same is true for FYROM (Former Yugoslav Republic of Macedonia), which is often listed among the members of the CEE group. In addition, some countries are (normally) included in the CEE group, although they are not European states in the geographical sense. Kazakhstan, Armenia and Georgia, all members of the CIS, provide suitable examples. The exclusion of the FR Yugoslavia, Croatia, and Bosnia and Herzegovina from the membership in this group causes further confusion regarding the structure of the CEE group, since they are located geographically in Central or Eastern Europe and are encircled by other members of the CEE group. There are obvious political reasons why these definitional blindspots were operating in the past, but in the future it would be appropriate to connect these countries to CEE or some other less inclusive set of countries for the purpose of the discourse about the future integration efforts in Europe as a whole.

Apart from the general transition process from non-market to market economies and from non-democratic to democratic political communities there is practically no significant 'common denominator' to the nations which belong to the CEE group. Not even their Communist past could underwrite attempts at partial homogenization. It is well-known that with the exceptions of Slovenia (which means also a piece of ex-Yugoslavia) and Albania, all the other CEE countries were parts of the past Soviet empire. They also participated in the CMEA economic integration. These facts, however, do not imply that there was a noticeable extent of economic or other homogenization among the CEE nations. There remained significant economic, historical and cultural differences until the present time. Some of the economic policies which were implemented in the past had even deepened the differences among the CEE countries. Before the beginning of the transition process the most significant differences among the CEE countries may have been induced by the considerably different structure of their individual foreign trade policies.

The seventies and eighties were characterised by a substantial diversity in economic policies among the CEE countries. The Baltic states, for example, were in fact part of the Soviet Union, sharing the specificities of that economic and political system. Hungary, in contrast, was (formally) a sovereign state which was introducing economic reforms and focusing on the gradual opening of the economy—within the limits set by the state ownership of 'means of production'. Romania, and to some extent Bulgaria, was replicating the economic system of the Soviet Union, engaged in sweeping economic policies which created a high level of economic dependence on the Soviet economy. In Poland and in Czechoslovakia, as in the other countries from the CEE group, the shares of export and import realized within the CMEA (and mostly with the Soviet Union) were extremely high. Slovenia—as a part of Yugoslavia, together with the newly emerged states in that area—was, in contrast to all the other CEE states, a much more market-based economy. With its relatively open economy—state monopoly in foreign trade was in fact more or less just symbolic and formal—Slovenia had an easier start on the new way towards the development of a fully-fledged market economy.

The individual CEE countries have succeeded in developing their contractual relations with the EU with different speed and on different formal grounds. The first countries which managed to conclude their EAAs were the Visegrad countries (Poland, Czechoslovakia, Hungary), followed by another five nations, while Slovenia was the last one in this specific group of ten CEE countries. The formal procedures to the conclusion of the EAAs were different, too. The Baltic states, for example, had for a short period Free Trade Agreements (FTA) with the EU, before concluding their EAAs. Slovenia had from 1992 to June 1996 an 'Economic Cooperation Agreement' with the EU. Other CEE countries were able to conclude their EAA directly. In the middle of 1996 it could not be reasonably expected that the number of countries with EAA will be increased at all in the foreseeable future. It is especially unlikely that such agreements could be signed between the EU and the countries from the CIS group. A little bit more uncertain is the position of the countries emerging from the ex-Yugoslavia (with the exception of Slovenia). It is then reasonable to state that aspirations for full membership in the EU are limited to the CEE countries with an EAA already concluded.

The institutional, historical, economic and other differences among the CEE countries disappear, however, when the interest of reaching a full membership in the EU is considered. Each CEE country is interested in integrating into the EU as full members in the relatively near future. Such aspirations are well-aligned with the on-going process of European integration, with the likely impacts of the increasingly liberalized international trade on economic development in Europe, and with other standard political and security interests. The motives of the CEE countries for gaining membership in the EU are to some extent conditioned on their individual differences. Besides their various history with the signing of the EAA, the CEE countries differ as well with respect to the way they expressed their political will for achieving full membership in the EU.

Formally, it was Hungary and Poland which applied first for membership in the EU, in 1994. In 1995, an additional four countries requested full membership in the EU. There are other countries which expect to be in the EU, but these have not yet decided to deliver their requests, only inscribed this wish in their individual EEA. Slovenia is an exception again, which submitted its request at the moment of signing the EAA. Formal requests for membership are important signs of political cohesion in a country where interests and obligations connected to the future steps of accession to the EU are considered.

2.3   Options for Integration and Their Relative Merits

For each country in CEE, as well as for the region as a whole, a number of fundamental options are available, which relate both to the economic and the political aspects of their relations with other European countries.

A. A country could abstain from all types of economic and/or political integration agreements.

B. A country may examine the effects of an eventual re-establishment of integration relations in the area of the former CMEA, or ex-Yugoslavia.

C. A country may consider establishing economic and/or political relations with some regional integration group outside Europe.

D. A country may think of adopting the development strategy of the 'Asian Tigers', and/or introducing the policy of off-shore centres.

E. A country may tend to accept a less demanding form of integration, like a Free Trade Agreement (FTA).

F. A country may decide to follow the goal of a fully-fledged EU accession.

Each of these options has some chance to be implemented in the case of CEE. Most of the options have been occasionally considered in professional or political circles in the CEE countries. It is obvious that the feasibility of the implementation of the above options varies, and is determined by the economic developments and political orientation of the individual CEE countries. There are also considerable differences in what the general public opinion is on each of the above potential development options.

Options B and C could be regarded as totally unrealistic for the majority of the CEE countries (excluding the CIS countries). The reorientation of trade towards the EU in the last years, the immediate effects of the signing of the EAAs, memories the economic inefficiency within the CMEA or ex-Yugoslavia: these are just some of the non-disputable reasons for option B to be unrealistic. But economic and political 'realism' about the acceptance of options B and C is not entirely in line with certain opinions of the public in some cases. In some CEE countries, a rather significant proportion of the answers to the question 'where does the future of our country lie?' was pointing to Russia. These countries were Bulgaria (23%), Estonia (17%), Latvia (24%), Lithuania (16%) (Eurobarometer, 1996 pp. 38–40). In a way, such responses could be interpreted as a (limited) interest for the re-establishment, in some form, of the erstwhile CMEA.

Option C for CEE is rather unfeasible for geographic reasons, which has an important impact on integration efforts and achievements. It is certainly true that, globally, the majority of the presently active and economically successful integrations include states which are related in geographic terms (WTO, 1995, p. 26). Geographical proximity is still among the key membership factors for all major integration groups world-wide. Normally, regional integration groups have no formal barriers to the entry of non-regional members. In principle, such membership could produce similar effects as the inclusion of members from the particular region. The benefits of such a non-regional integration, however, could be substantially reduced by the relatively higher transportation costs and the potentially more significant linguistic, cultural, legal and other differences. Therefore, from a practical point of view, option C is not a feasible alternative. But one can find some support among the general public of the CEE countries for this option as well.

A certain part of the public is inclined to believe that the future for their country lies in closer links with the United States of America, for example; in Hungary (15%), in Slovenia (15%), in Poland (14%), in Slovakia (13%), and in Romania (32%) (Eurobarometer '96, pp. 38–40). It should be noted that such opinions are in fact not focused on integration with any other country outside of Europe. They are connected solely to the United States. This fact and another, that the public preference for that option is much weaker than that for option F, still support the view that option C is not in fact an acceptable or practical alternative for CEE. This conclusion cannot be challenged by the somewhat surprising result achieved in Romania. In Romania, in fact, a slightly stronger public interest is expressed for closer relations with the United States (32%) than with the EU (30%).

Option A is no doubt an operationally feasible solution for each CEE country. In our times of economic globalization and liberalization, however, it is a rather unrealistic option. Technological progress and frequent changes in the factors which determine competitiveness on various markets impose an ever growing need for the expansion of foreign trade. Option A, due to the necessity of accelerating economic development based on the growth of foreign trade (in goods, in services, in capital flows), is in fact a rather unacceptable option for each CEE country. The majority of the CEE countries have relatively small economies, and are not able to sustain a relatively high growth rate by means of protectionism. Besides economic integration, only a general and radical foreign trade liberalization could support faster economic growth. Outward-looking development is promising both by theoretical considerations and on the ground of the experience with global liberalization. Once they have, inevitably, rejected option A, the CEE countries need to evaluate the development model exercised in the last decades by the so-called 'Asian Tigers' (option D).

Option D comes with the adoption of an economic policy which is based on the principles of export-led growth and the utilization of dynamic comparative advantages. An eventual subscription to the 'Asian Tigers' development model would force the individual CEE countries to follow broader external trade liberalization policies (in order to avoid discrimination), compared to ones demanded by any sort of regional integration agreement. In the case of integration, foreign trade liberalization policies are limited to the participating countries only, so they have a much smaller impact on the country's economic openness. The 'Asian Tigers' model may be more attractive than the integration option. If it was eventually accepted by any CEE country, one of the benefits it could bring is the possibility of buying on the cheapest markets of the world. Usually trade partners which belong to the same integration are not in fact the cheapest potential suppliers. Allocation of resources could also be suboptimal due to the limited competition within the integration. The decision concerning option D is not as straightforward as in the case of the other possible options for CEE. As a rule, the official political stance of the CEE governments and public opinion as well point to enhanced integration with the EU instead of realizing the otherwise feasible option of imitating the development policy pattern of the 'Asian Tigers'.

The remaining options, E and F, are both acceptable for CEE, on the bases of politics, economics and the opinions of the public. The exact choice between the options should depend mainly on the internal economic and political goals of the CEE countries and on the actual intensity of the EU's interest in enlargement. If we mark the interest of the CEE countries in full accession to the EU by AA (for 'aspiration to accession') and the interest of the EU to incorporate countries from the CEE group by IE ('interest to enlarge'), we can construct the following simple chart representing the preference for either of the two options:

$$AA = IE \quad (1)$$
$$AA > IE \quad (2)$$
$$AA < IE \quad (3).$$

In case (1) the selection of option F is highly probable. In case (2) expectations of the CEE countries would turn out to be too high, which means that solution F could not be implementable in practice. Case (3) is at the moment not entirely realistic. In the EU, intentions to enlarge the integration are confronted with intentions to deepen it. The deliberations of the EU inter-governmental conference, which is to discuss, among others, the issue of future enlargement will not be known until the end of 1996 or even as late as 1997. For the time being, the scenario expressed by relation (3) can be reasonably regarded as unrealistic.

On the basis of the evidence of the Eurobarometer '96, the public in CEE is generally inclined to believe that the economic and political success of their country is closely related to forging closer ties to the EU, although this belief should not be seen as steady. In the countries which have concluded their EAAs, 34% of the people which were interviewed in 1994 and 1995 expressed the opinion that the development of their country is decisively affected by their relations with the EU, rather than with the United States (16%), Russia (9%), the Central and Eastern European countries (8%) and Germany (6%). Public opinion varies substantially among the CEE countries regarding the importance of the EU for their future development, from the highest in Estonia (45%) and Slovenia (44%), to the lowest in Lithuania (30%) and Hungary (26%).

Public opinion and, as well, some theoretical considerations support the claim that option E is not to be entirely neglected. Option E seems to be preferable especially in the cases when its acceptance does not forestall the realization of option F. Option E has been already partially implemented by the erection of the Central European Free Trade Area (CEFTA). Obviously, integration agreements on the bases of FTA among CEE countries could not be regarded as a potential substitute to the option of full membership in the EU. In fact such integration agreements can only facilitate economic progress to the extent to which they support the full membership of the CEE countries in the EU. At present, the situation is closer to the relation expressed by (2) than by (1). Somehow, the deflated interest on the part of the EU countries is grounded in some predominantly static evaluations of the expected effects of the enlargement. Among others, the future net outflow from the EU budget in the direction of the new EU members is cited the most (Appendix 3, Table 1). Only by offering a more dynamic assessment of the enlargement process can the positions of the two parties be brought closer to the relation expressed in equation (1) above.

Although the CEE countries are on average more intensively interested in membership in the EU than are the present members of the EU in its (fast) enlargement, noticeable differences can be detected in both groups. In CEE, aspiration for accession and full membership, as expressed in public opinion polls, is often negatively related to the realized level and intensity of (economic) relations. It has to be noticed that accession aspirations are as a rule in decline whenever the level and complexity of cooperation with the EU is increased. 'People are positive rather than negative about the aims and activities of the European Union, despite a slight deterioration in the image of the EU throughout the region surveyed' (Eurobarometer '96, p. 42). In four of the ten EAA countries the reputation of the EU has regressed since the previous Eurobarometer survey; these are Lithuania (–11%), Bulgaria (–10%), the Czech Republic (–8) and Slovakia (–6%). In the past four years, the most pronounced deterioration in the perception of the EU has occurred in Lithuania, where 51%

of those asked had a favorable picture of the EU in 1992, compared to 23% at the beginning of 1996. Five countries have remained rather stable regarding the image of the EU (Latvia, Estonia, Hungary, Romania), only in Poland has the image slightly increased (+4%).

The positive image of the EU, and the related relatively high public interest in the access to the Union, is based on economic expectations. Expectations of positive political or security impacts of the EAA for the CEE countries are not so dominant. The importance attached to the economic impact of the accession on CEE could also be illustrated by surveying what may be behind the negative expectations related to the accession to the Union. 'A negative view of the Union is often based on a conviction that their own country will be exploited economically or that the national economy will lose out because it is too weak' (Eurobarometer '96, p. 53). What concerns these negative aspects, the causes of reservations are relatively similar for both groups of countries.

The opening of the CEE markets, initiated by the implementation of the EAAs, have already induced some economic effects which are not perceived favourably by the public, these include increased domestic competition and the otherwise 'necessary' restructuring of production activities. The compensation effects of the different EU support programmes (PHARE, TEMPUS) and of the slow process of the opening of the CEE markets, are not strong enough to countervail the growing reservations regarding further integration with the EU. This can be illustrated by citing the following opinions: 'People in Hungary for example say, describing their partners from the EU, "they are looking to sell, not to buy"; and in Latvia "our production will be ruined given that our products do not conform to European standards"' (Eurobarometer '96, p. 53). It is certain that there are going to be short-term negative effects on both sides, distributed across different production sectors. It could as well be added that the relative 'volume' of short-term negative economic impacts for CEE will generally exceed the 'volume' of such impacts in the EU member countries. The opening of markets on both sides, in spite of the asymmetry in its implementation, has produced some supply effects; on the markets of individual CEE countries these are comparable to a flood, while in the EU the effect could be compared to a barely noticable stream.

In CEE, the importance of economic effects for the level of intensity with which accession is desired is further related to expectations of the public concerning economic development. It is an often expressed opinion that future economic progress in a country from the CEE group will in fact be arranged by a future membership in the Union. For example, Croatia (23%) and Albania (17%) expect the most from additional inflows of development aid which is supposed to follow an eventual EU membership. Both examples support the above expressed claim: expectations of beneficial effects from the EU accession are generally much higher in those countries where the formal and the *de facto* level of economic relations with the EU is in fact lower.

2.4   Integration and Economic Growth

Above, we have tried to indicate that, on the one hand, the individual CEE countries have rather different outlooks on the timing and structure of the accession process, while on the other hand, the EU and the CEE countries also have divergent expectations concerning the enlargement. These differences are strongly determined by the actual and expected economic results which accompany or follow the accession process. But neither scepticism nor euphoria are acceptable while one considers the pros and cons of a possible future integration step to be taken by the EU or CEE. Let us, then, briefly reflect on the potential economic effects of the liberalization of mutual trade flows (of goods, services and capital).

Economists know that it is difficult, if not impossible, to find an ideal solution for a given problem, the sort of solution which has no negative effects besides the major positive one. Economic choices are based on the different interests of the economic agents and on the deviations of the actual performance of markets from the ideal: a situation in which there is an unlimited number of agents on a market, products are homogenous, there is 'perfect' information about the relevant variables, there is no interference with the market on the part of the state, and last but not least, all participants are unfailingly rational.

In practical life, theoretical conditions tend not to be fulfilled. The motivation for the liberalization of international trade in general or in the context of a regional integration can be seen as an effort to assimilate actual market conditions as close as possible to the standard theoretical assumptions.

Discussions of international trade liberalization provide an excellent opportunity for a dispute among economists and different economic agents, some of whom are in favour of trade liberalization in general or in a regional context and those who oppose it. These disputes may start with assertions that the likely effects of liberalization will differ substantially from what can be expected theoretically. It can proceed to arguing about the unequal distribution of potential benefits among the owners of various production factors and among the states which participate in the process. It can be, in addition, specifically argued, for instance, that liberalization will deliver more gains to the partners with better initial positions and to the more developed states than to other participants. All of these various doubts and concerns can appear while the issue of accession to the EU is debated.

The disputes may continue with challenging the correctness of theoretical explanations of comparative advantages among countries, advantages which accrue to production specialization. There are many other ways in which some disputants could disagree with the idea that in a longer period all participants in general or regional trade liberalization could realize positive gains. As we already pointed out, the expected effects of accession to the EU might as well be publicly interpreted as a danger for the less developed members of CEE. It could also be argued that something similar can develop among the EU members.

The assessment of the benefits and costs resulting from general or regional trade liberalization is often based on the comparison of relative comparative advantages between the countries which are parts of the liberalization efforts. Comparative advantages are usually determined at a single point in time, but long-term benefits of specialization in production depend a great deal on their *dynamic* effects on an economy. But there is no method for the evaluation of the dynamic effects of trade liberalization on an economy to which all the economists and public policy experts would subscribe.

Paul Krugman has constructed a formal model to explain the potentially negative effect of liberalization among countries which are characterized by different dynamic quality of comparative advantages. After attributing external economies to the industrial sector, he claimed that '[the] process [under scrutiny]... captures the essence of the argument that trade with developed nations prevents industrialization in less developed countries' (Krugman, 1990, p. 93). There are some other academic studies dealing with growth theory which tend to support this kind of reasoning. The model developed by Robert Lucas, for example, emphasizes the importance of initial conditions for future development: 'an economy beginning with low levels of human and physical capital will remain permanently below the performance of an initially better-endowed economy' (Lucas, 1988, p. 25). Robert Solow, in a review article on growth theory, suggested: '[Lucas'] particular model suggests, although it does not quite imply, that the countries specializing in high technology will grow faster than the others and thus reinforce their comparative advantage' (Solow, 1991, p. 407).

The reasoning expressed in the above academic observations, in combination with some pieces of practical evidence from the past EU development (the lagging development of Greece, for example), could provoke a great deal of concern on the side of relatively less developed CEE countries. Concerns of the CEE economies regarding further accession could be explained by the fact that the complex, although gradual, process of integration with the EU introduces complete and reciprocal external liberalization with respect to the more developed countries of the EU.

The dilemma described is not new and in fact some rather convincing practical and theoretical evidence could be invoked to prove that there are positive development effects of moves towards gradual and selective external economic liberalization in less developed economies. An often used example of controlled and selective liberalization is the case of the Newly Industrialised Countries, among them the well-known group of 'Asian Tigers'. They succeeded to make a 'jump' from low skilled labour production to production of high-tech products by the help of intensive development of their international trade. Gradual and controlled foreign trade liberalization was not supported or demanded, in their case, by any type of trade liberalization imposed by regional integration activities. Their achievements suggest that even countries with lower development levels could succeed, through a process of economic opening and liberalization, in catching up with the more advanced economies. Comparative advantages obviously change dynamically and thus liberalization in countries with lower development levels could still support a desirable change in production structure and could induce real economic achievements: in economic growth, in the level of employment and in terms of technological change. The Asian Tigers have actually proved that comparative advantage can in fact be turned around. These experiences suggest that integration with the EU would not necessarily lead to a situation in which the CEE countries would persist in lagging behind the EU countries in terms of economic development.

Liberalization based on accession to the EU could be acceptable for CEE in spite of the differences in development and comparative advantages. 'Thus, with free mobility of factors of production, comparative advantage becomes a much less relevant concept, because factors from different countries will instead flow across borders according to the logic of absolute advantage' (Ekins, 1993, p. 3). Besides trade liberalization, another crucial prerequisite for the successful conclusion of the accession process is an effective parallel implementation of the free movement of labour and capital between the EU and the accessing CEE countries. The interests of the CEE countries to become full members of the EU are grounded not only in the expected introduction of free mobility of production factors within the EU. An additional impetus for the strive for full membership in the EU is generated by the need to react to the changing global economic environment.

One of the principal trends in the world today can be captured by the word 'globalization', which engages many aspects of contemporary life: culture, communication, environmental concerns, trade and competition. All these have increasingly global dimensions.

But this trend is perhaps most significant in the realm of economics. Between 1950 and the beginning of the present decade, world trade increased 11 times, to over 3.5 trillion 1990 US dollars, over twice as fast as world product which increased by nearly five times over the same period.

Large transnational corporations, economically integrated states and more and more global international economic organizations, such as the World Trade Organisation (WTO), became the major powers in the world economy of today.

The importance of these big international players is well known. By 1990, the turnover of one of the world's largest corporations, General Motors, was nearly equal to the world's 21st largest GDP, that of Australia. The turnover of each of the world's largest corporations exceeded the individual GDP of more than half of the world's national-states (Fortune, 1990), including the CEE countries. In a discussion of economic integration among national-states, one may also mention that in 1993 more than 44% of the merchandise exports of the world originated in Western Europe. Two integrations—the European Union and the European Free Trade Area (EFTA) combined into the European Economic Area (EEA)—are the leading powers in international trade.

For the CEE countries, it is reasonable to follow the principle of ever closer economic integration with the leading global trading area developed in their neighbourhood. Efforts of the CEE countries to prepare for full membership in the EU, in the sense of opening their markets to the competition from these countries, will be reinforced by their obligations to the World Trade Organisation. The demands of following the liberalization 'schedules' in the trade of all goods and services will additionally accelerate the growth of competition on the national markets of CEE. That way, the task of the CEE countries to prepare for full membership in the EU will be an even more challenging and demanding process. There is, however, no alternative which could further more the future successful economic development and growth of the CEE countries.

2.5   Coming to Terms With the Accession I

The first step in the accession process is the fulfilment of the necessary requirements for the integration into the internal market of the Union. Some rather general first criteria were set at the Copenhagen Summit in June 1993. They were issued on the assumption that these criteria have to be met by the CEE countries before they would become new members of the EU. At the Essen Summit in December 1994, a comprehensive strategy for the accession of the CEE countries was formulated on the basis of these criteria. It was more operational and outlined the adjustment steps which have to be taken by the CEE countries in the process of accession. A further elaboration of the accession strategy was formulated in the White Paper. It was formally approved at the Summit in Cannes in June 1995.

The White Paper has set the guidelines for the integration of CEE into the single market. These call for the development of an environment for the free movement of goods, services, people and capital between the EU and the countries with an EAA. The recommendations of the White Paper do not have to be followed by the EAA countries and it does not promise a future accession into the EU, either.

On the basis of the previously accepted set of documents, which dealt with the conditions of the accession and the necessary adjustments to be made before its completion, the Commission of the EU distributed a special Questionnaire to the CEE countries with an EAA in the Spring of 1996. The purpose of the Questionnaire is the assessment of the present level of preparation of the CEE countries in those key areas which are the most important for their successful

Table 1 Accession criteria and their perception based on different expectations of benefits and costs of the accession process

		perception of the criteria			
		in the EU authorities		in the CEE authorities	
	Union	members states	groups*	in CEE states	groups*
Acc. criteria as a barrier	no	some	some	yes	mostly yes
Acc. criteria as a support tool	yes	some	yes	no	some

* groups: industries, political parties, production factors owners.

integration into the EU. The answers of the CEE countries were to be prepared and returned to the Commission by the end of July 1996.

The entire process described above, by which the EU issued declarations and documents concerning the future enlargement with the CEE countries, differed considerably from the practices used in the past when enlargements had been considered. This situation creates worries and uncertainty on the part of the 'accessing' countries, since from their point of view all these documents and activities could be no more than a cover for an insufficient (or even no) interest of the EU to adopt new members. The unprecedented act of formulating and gradually elaborating criteria for the accession could be interpreted by the CEE countries in two different ways.

First, the process of criteria elaboration could be comprehended as a development of a new instrument invented for the management of the complex and demanding process of integration. Second, on the contrary, this process could as well be viewed as a manoeuvre for a gradual erection of a major barrier towards the future accession of the CEE countries into the EU.

Due to the different economic, political and security interests in CEE and in the EU, there cannot be a uniform answer to this dilemma, due to the numerous alternative perspectives on the situation. For the sake of the final success of the accession process, it is also important to note that the interpretation of the criteria is as much diversified among interest groups within the EU as they are among the various interest groups within an individual CEE country. The diverging views on the role of the criteria in the accession process reflect the different perceptions of the potential benefits and costs accruing to the several partners participating in this process.

The perception of the accession criteria is quite different in the EU and in CEE. In the EU, among the groups which may wish to regard the accession criteria as a barrier for the new members are mainly industries which use predominantly unskilled or low skilled labour. This observation can be supported by analyses of the sensitivity of the relevant production sectors on the completion of the integration process, and on studies of the expected impact on factor endowments (European Commission, 1994). In some EU member states, using the accession criteria as potential barriers to enlargement could be favoured by producers in (specific) agricultural sectors (grain production, for example). It is often argued that the funds needed for coping with the agricultural sector in CEE would reduce the financial support which this same sector receives in the present member states, or, otherwise, the EU budget will be ruined. Robert Baldwin has calculated that the associated costs would reach ECU 38 billion only for the four Visegrad countries (Baldwin, 1994). Besides some production sectors, some EU member countries may be inclined to oppose accession *en bloc*; some of the less developed members of the EU (Portugal, Greece or Spain) could potentially urge the understanding of the accession criteria as a (convenient) barrier to the enlargement.

Practically without exception, the authorities in CEE regard the accession criteria as an unavoidable obstacle on their way to future membership in the EU. Often the same attitude is favoured by a number of professional economists from CEE (Inotai, 1995). 'For the first time, specific conditions are being imposed on acceding countries, whereas the Treaty of Rome laid down only the one condition that an entrant country must be European. So the Copenhagen decision in fact constitutes an act of discrimination against the transitional countries' (Inotai, 1994).

In CEE, political parties in power, and even some opposition parties, often understand accession criteria, together with the continuous evolution of their contents, as a major barrier to the future membership of their countries in the EU. It is obvious that EU programmes for the support of the transition and of the accession are welcome by political parties and by governments. It is rather rare that political parties regard the criteria as factors which might facilitate enlargement. Only specific groups of institutions or individuals have a positive perception of the accession criteria, ones which are, for example, directly involved in the implementation of the specific programmes launched by the EU (cf. PHARE and other support programmes).

Differences in interpreting the actual role of the accession criteria in CEE and in the EU are closely related to the differentiated interpretations of two decisive issues surrounding the future economic and political integration in Europe. These two issues are the 'widening' of the EU and, in a kind of opposition to it, the 'deepening' of the present level of integration among EU members.

The inclusion of the time of the enlargement and of the level of membership into the discussion makes the evaluation of the opportunities of CEE to integrate successfully into the EU even more complex. It is obvious that behind the different expectations regarding the time and manner of accession lie differences in the actual economic and political positions of the individual countries and of the specific interest groups within those countries.

Looking for common motives for all the EU and CEE agents involved in the process of enlargement could be the only effective way to arrive at

Table 2 Difference in preceptions regarding future enlargement of the EU

		Position Demanded or Wished	
Time Member	Country Group	Full Member	Partial
Immediate Enlargement of the EU	CEE	Poland, Czech R., Hungary, Slovenia	No
	EU	No	No
Enlargement of the EU should be due rather **soon** (to the end of the Century)	CEE	Other countries with EAAs	Officially **No** (except for Slovenia*) **Yes** Some business and political options
	EU	No Proponents of the EU priority for the process of 'Deepening' EU relations	No Except for membership suggestion(s) limited to political and security pillars of the EU (Andrissen)
Later Enlargement (in 10 to 20 years)	CEE	No	No
	EU	**Yes** More defined position expected as a result of IC**	**Yes** Isolated groups and lobbies; agriculture, less developed areas and potentially some countries

* Slovenia has officially sought membership in the EFTA, during period of uncertainty about the perspective of signing the EAA. This solution was treated as a 'second best option' compared to full membership in the EU.

** Intergovernmental Conference of the EU member states (1996).

Source: Author's evaluations.

acceptable future accession criteria and the same holds for the task of achieving the necessary economic and legal harmonization within the CEE countries during the accession period. Searching for the common denominator of interests should be based on a cost-benefit analysis of the enlargement.

The EAA countries prefer an immediate or short-run realization of their full membership within the EU. Accession in the long-run—in 10 to 20 years—appears to them less than attractive. It could be argued that much of the reasoning behind this preference could be explained by the internal politics in the individual CEE countries. In the majority of the countries in transition, the EU has a highly positive image among the population.

In fact, 40% of those questioned (Eurobarometer, 1996, p. 42) in the EAA countries and in Slovenia have a positive image of the EU. A negative image of the EU is rare; it characterizes only 6% of the people interviewed. The distribution of positive and negative images of the EU varies among the CEE countries, but nevertheless, as a rule, the EU compares favourably with other countries or regional options. This positive image is based on the perception of the EU as an integration of well-to-do, politically stable and democratic societies. The expected and desired membership in the EU is often seen as a guarantee for the same favourable economic conditions and living-standards as is normal in the present EU member states, disregarding any limits potentially caused by the present differences in development levels. Such expectations, in a way, form a typical case of confusing the ends with the means. The generally accepted development goal of improving the economic and political conditions of the CEE group is thought to be securely achieved by the formal act of becoming a member of the EU. Membership in the EU is very often understood as a major goal in itself, which should be achieved as soon as possible. No doubt, faster economic and even political improvements in the CEE group could be achieved via the financial and other support mechanisms available for less developed countries and regions within the EU. But this potential benefit of membership in the EU should be compared with the costs of the initial adjustment in the CEE countries, together with the costs of enlargement for the EU. The debate is focused on whether the expected aggregate costs (for the EU and CEE together) would exceed the expected aggregate benefits if membership is enlarged sooner or later (see Table 2). The differences between the EU and CEE in assessing the proper time for enlargement clearly show that both sides have considerably different opinions about the costs and benefits of enlargement. The main outlines of the problem has already been elaborated above. Here, we would like to add some elements in order to understand better the difficult structure of the basic relations, which are important for the emergence of potentially matching interests between the two groups of countries.

The specific elements that further stimulate the differences in perception of acceptable (desired) moment and type of accession between CEE and the EU are connected to the internal political situation of the CEE countries.

The legacy of Communism combined with the sometimes sluggish economic progress had created a conducive environment for an enthusiastic perception of the EU achievements among the population of many Central and East European countries. Partial evidence for this is offered by the differences among the CEE countries regarding the European Union's positive image.

In each country (Table 3), the positive image of the EU has been declining in the last few years. The only exception to this rule is Poland. The general decline of positive image of the EU among peoples of CEE could be interpreted as a sign of better information and the gradual change in the former rather naive perceptions. Not so uniformly, but rather regularly, the ratio of positive images is higher in the countries with less actual trade or other relations with the EU. The examples are Albania and Romania. From this trend, Bulgaria seems to be the exception. Although the positive image of the EU is on the decline, as we noted earlier, in the majority of the countries the

Table 3   Changing image of the EU among the CEE countries (% of positive image responses)

	1992	1993	1994	1995
Albania	79	71	72	64
Bulgaria	51	42	37	27
Czech R.	45	37	34	26
Estonia	32	31	29	30
FYROM*	20	27	39	40
Hungary	34	36	32	30
Latvia	40	40	39	35
Lithuania	43	45	41	23
Poland	48	37	42	46
Romania	55	45	51	50
Slovakia	35	44	37	31
Slovenia	45	30	37	35

* FYROM; Former Yugoslav Republic of Macedonia

Source: Eurobarometer-Central and Eastern, No. 6, European Commission, 1996.

proportion of positive images is still higher than that of the negative ones.

For some governments and some political parties in the CEE group, presenting a generally positive image of the EU is highly attractive due to internal political reasons. Associating a particular government's or political party's actions with the positive perception of the EU could increase their popularity within the population. Beside economic, political and security reasons, this fact could offer an additional explanation for the fact that the combination of full membership with quick accession is the only acceptable or mostly favoured option among the CEE countries.

The preparation of the CEE countries for accession is influenced by the position explained above. Basically, it leads to the idea that the membership of the EU could be enlarged prior to the end of the adjustment process in protected sectors. After accession, a process of adjustment and harmonization could be continued in a similar way as was the practice in the past when new members were accepted. Members of the CEE group often use the example of the last instance of EU enlargement as a paradigm for their own case as well.

Differences among the present members of the EU about the time for enlargement often involve budgetary issues. Countries with net contribution into the EU budget tend to advocate enlargement after elimination of major development differences. The countries that support most openly the idea of enlargement after the end of transition—probably after the realization of the content of the EAA—are Germany, France, Austria, Sweden and Finland. In each case, this can be traced back to their specific economic interests. The less developed members of the EU (Appendix 3, Table 1) are in general rather reluctant or even reserved regarding the potential enlargement of the EU, which is due to the possibility of the reorientation of financial support to the newcomers. They defend the option of later EU enlargement combined with the request for prior complete fulfilment of enlargement criteria.

2.6   Coming to Terms With the Accession II

Construing the accession criteria either as a barrier for the accessing countries or as a support tool for enlargement is equally wrong. They are predominantly the necessary harmonization elements which can secure the successful long-term existence of the future enlarged integration of the EU. The theory of economic integration (Kumar, 1995) and evidence about the failures of numerous integrations, for example in Africa and Latin America, support the view that the fulfilment of a minimum level of convergence among integrating countries is a necessity (Barro, 1991; Baumol, 1986). More complex levels of integration, e.g., from a Free Trade Area to an internal market, require higher levels of convergence among the partner countries. Only that can make the higher level of integration stable, really effective and beneficial to all members in the long run.

The enlargement of the EU with the members from the CEE group is even more demanding, regarding the necessary level of convergence among old and new integration partners. At present, the EU features an integration whose structure differs from any other known type of integration. The requirements to be fulfilled by members or potential new members in the area of economic and legal harmonization (maintaining or developing a proper level of convergence) far exceed the requirements at the level of the internal market. The EU as an integration automatically demands from new members, to prepare for the integration not only in the economic sphere, but on the political and security levels as well. This increases the level of convergence among old and potential new members. Only a higher level of convergence could support the successful functioning of the enlarged integration, securing the expected benefits to both old and to new members.

The debate on whether the accession criteria function as an integration tool or as a barrier to potential members is related to the dilemma of when exactly the criteria should be fulfilled by the potential new members of the EU. There are three possible time options for the fulfilment of the accession criteria. These could be reasonably discussed only when the accession criteria are not construed as an entry barrier to new members and if they are not unnecessarily excessive and demanding in their formal structure in the 1995 White Paper.

Accession criteria may be fulfilled by the CEE countries before entering the EU. Possibly they can be fulfilled after entering into the EU membership within an agreed period. The third alternative is a partial solution; the vital criteria should be met before the EU enlargement and the rest after that. Accepting the third alternative brings forward the question whether the pre-accession criteria are too extensive and demanding in their present form.

Which of the above alternatives is more advantageous for the CEE countries depends on numerous factors. This can be illustrated by the metaphor of ten passengers trying to catch a train pulling out from the station. All passengers might catch the train, or only some, or even none of them. The task of the passengers is even more demanding due to the acceleration of the train. It requires more and more effort from the runners and the available time for catching the train is getting shorter. It becomes especially short if there is no chance that the driver will eventually slow down to pick up (some of) the passengers. The ten CEE countries which concluded the EAAs are in exactly the same position towards the EU enlargement as the ten passengers trying to catch the train. The individual passenger's (country's) chances of catching the train depend upon the level of physical fitness (higher level of convergence). Their potential for catching the train in fact depends on the quality of the past training (economic performance). Some weaker passengers (states with lower convergence), having had less training in the past (slower transition), could hope to be pulled forward by stronger passengers (partners from CEE). Such a solution could be a good hope for the less advanced countries, but it is at the same time a dangerous decision for fitter countries. The additional burden of dragging along less able passengers can substantially reduce their chances of catching the running train of the EU.

Coming back to the problem of the CEE countries, they might help each other to get better results of convergence development with the EU, but the energy devoted to that purpose could delay them in fulfilling the accession criteria in proper time for the EU enlargement.

Due to the substantial differences in economic development, and because of the noticeable differences in the results of the transition and the catching up processes the chances of the individual countries to catch the accelerating train of the EU are different. Even the available support forms from the EU are most probably not intensive enough to eliminate those major differences in a short time. The position of CEE is similar to the situation of the passengers. They cannot run much faster if some passers-by start to stimulate them by shouting. Such supports might be stimulating, but catching the train will in fact still depend on previous training in running and additionally on the actual acceleration rate of the train. Let us think for a moment what options are open to the CEE countries to improve their economic position and other necessary elements to be better and sooner prepared for membership in the EU.

2.7 Development Alternatives of Catching Up With the EU

Implementation of the EAA have introduced a process of substantial changes in the CEE countries' economic growth potential. The enhanced competition on their national markets introduced relatively complex production restructuring. The increased openness of the CEE countries, based on implementation of the EAA, has initiated a noticeable decrease in their budgetary income based on import duties.

An important dilemma for the partners in the accession process is whether it is possible for the CEE countries to reach and maintain relatively high economic growth rates (over 4%) over a long period of time. According to some estimates, this is the growth rate necessary to secure the gradual closing of the present development gap. This dilemma cannot be answered directly, in spite of the numerous research done in this area. What can be reasonably expected is that high economic growth rates are feasible for periods of 10 to maybe 15 years.

The past economic growth achieved by the countries called the 'Asian Tigers' (Hong Kong, South Korea, Singapore and Taiwan) supports the idea that high growth rates are possible to achieve as well in the case of CEE. The usefulness of the case of the Asian countries for assessing the development perspective of CEE is in some respects quite limited. First of all, as it has been mentioned, the Asian counties have succeeded in achieving high growth rates without any foreign trade liberalization imposed by an economic integration agreement (except Singapore, which is a member of the ASEAN free trade area). Their case proves only the fact that for less developed countries high, long-term and stable growth rates are achievable, together with the reasonable chance for gradually closing the development gap in relation to the most developed countries.

The Asian countries have started, like the CEE countries, their successful economic progress from low levels of industrialization and GDP per capita. From that starting point they have managed to achieve approximately 7% average growth rate of the GDP per capita on a yearly basis. They succeeded in maintaining this very high growth rate in the long period from 1960 to 1990 (Baldwin, 1993). The precondition for achieving such high growth rates was a combination of their gradual liberalization of imports and the simultaneous implementation of an industrial policy, which was based on export-led growth principles. The expansion of exports was one of the major factors supporting the sustainability of high growth rates. The annual level of exports of these countries rose annually by 15% on average in the period between 1970 and 1990 (Baldwin, 1993).

The success of the Asian countries in closing (in 20 years) the development gap—which was extremely large initially—suggests some lessons for the CEE countries too.

For CEE, considering the relevance of the development experiences of the successful Asian countries, the following question could be raised. How can the integration activities—among themselves and (or) with the EU—influence their present efforts in closing the development gap with the EU? The case of fast developing Asian countries implicity suggests that the implementation of integration relations among the countries is in fact not a necessary precondition for secure and fast sustainable economic growth. It could be argued however, following theoretical works and on the bases of the past EU development experiences, that a properly prepared and monitored integration process could increase the chances of sustainable and relatively fast economic growth in the CEE countries. Integration with the EU could be interpreted and used as a facilitation instrument to support additional acceleration of economic growth in the CEE countries.

The accession requirements, reflecting the content of the 1995 White Paper, could be, from this aspect, considered a necessary tool for successful integration of the CEE countries into the EU. The tool nature of the requirements is acknowledged especially by the explicit form of the 1995 White Paper, which is a recommendation. During the process of implementing the accession criteria a structured dialogue between the EU and potential new members should help to adjust accession requirements according to specific characteristics of the CEE countries. An active role of the CEE countries in that process, based on their evaluations of expected economic effects of the requirements implementation, is in fact essential for the successful accomplishment of their accession to the EU.

In the CEFTA countries, together with Lithuania and Estonia, economic growth have been positive in the last two years. Positive economic growth is an important achievement in the efforts of catching up with the EU development level. Nevertheless, substantial differences have been recorded in the economic growth rates of the CEE countries with EAA. In 1995, the lowest positive growth rates were recorded in Estonia and Hungary (close to zero). Among the CEE countries Poland had recorded the highest growth rate (7%) for 1995. Differences in growth rates combined with substantial differences of the initial levels of respective GDPs still point to a difference among the CEE countries regarding the time necessary for catching up with the EU, on the basis of GDP.

It could be argued that the estimates of Baldwin, 1993 and 1994 are not entirely correct regarding the time necessary for reaching the 75% of the average EU GDP by the CEE countries. For the four original CEFTA countries the 20 years calculated by Baldwin may be in fact be too long. But even if, for example, the necessary time is in fact substantially shorter, it is still obvious that major differences exist among the individual CEE countries regarding the 'threshold' level. This is true notwithstanding the various suggestions that perhaps the calculation of the actual level of GDP in CEE was not correct, due to the exclusion of the impact of long-term trends of currency appreciation caused by large efficiency gains (Rosati, 1995), or that GDP level calculations have not included the effects of shadow or grey economy in the countries in transition. For example, in Poland the shadow economy is estimated at about 20% of the officially registered activities, and the situation is similar in other CEE countries (Kawecka, 1996).

These exclusions and the observed specific characteristics could in fact change the assessment of the starting GDP level of individual CEE countries considerably. This brings us to some additional shortening of the assumed time for reaching 75% of the average EU GDP. This fact per se could not be properly used as an argument for an immediate or quick accession of the CEE group to the EU. The problem of accession is not limited to the dilemma of proper timing of the enlargement, but it also entails the problem of different development rate of the individual countries. Here, an additional dilemma can be formulated. Is it essential for the benefit of the EU and of the new potential members that they join the integration only after reaching the relevant levels of economic development, sustainable growth and stability? Before trying to answer this well known question, usually answered in opposite ways in the CEE group and in the EU, we would like to reflect on some other development results for the countries with EAAs.

Inflation was a major problem among the CEE countries at the beginning of the transition process. Beside their economic potential, measured by GDP level and growth rate, inflation is an important indicator of the countries' ability to access the EU. In addition, the inflation rate is one of the accepted criteria for the future Monetary Union membership.

In the last few years, the fight against inflation has produced rather different results in the individual CEE countries. By 1995, a small group of countries succeeded in pushing the annual inflation rate below the 10% mark: Slovenia, the Czech Republic and Slovakia. The second and larger group of countries with the EAA was not equally successful in controlling inflation. They have yearly inflation rates above the 20% mark: Poland, Latvia, Rumania, Hungary and Estonia. In 1995 Bulgaria and Lithuania were even over the 30% mark.

The restructuring of the CEE economies was connected to an increase in unemployment rates. Unemployment is a relatively substantial problem for CEE. In the larger group of these countries, Poland, Bulgaria, Slovakia, Lithuania and Hungary, the unemployment rate was over 10% in the last two years. The group which had unemployment rate below 10% consists of two countries with low levels of unemployment, below 6%, the Czech Republic and Estonia, and the other two, Slovenia and Latvia, have unemployment rates between 6 and 10%. From the point of view of development, it is interesting to note that low levels of monthly wages in the CEE countries are not necessary connected to lower rates of unemployment. Bulgaria and Slovakia have rather high unemployment rates, although they have at the same time the lowest levels of monthly wages. In contrast, the relatively high level of wages in Slovenia is not connected with the relatively highest level of unemployment (Appendix 2, Table 1).

In the case of the CEE countries with the concluded EAAs, the impacts of trade liberalization has been temporarily asymmetric in favour of the CEE countries. To the surprise of many analysts, this temporary asymmetry in bilateral trade failed to provide the CEE countries with a sustainable surplus. After an initial boom of exports caused by a number of domestic and external factors, their imports from the EU started to grow faster than their exports. It could be said that the 'development asymmetry' proved stronger than the temporary and rather selective 'trade asymmetry'. It is an inevitable result that practically all CEE countries experienced a growing trade deficit with the EU. The future stability of trade liberalization, as an important part of EAA realization, largely depends on the capacity of CEE to finance the growing trade deficit with the EU. Liberalization of trade as a part of the EAA concept is additionally endangered by the fact that the majority of the CEE countries with EAA have recorded a growing current account deficit in the last few years. Only Slovenia, Bulgaria and Slovakia have recorded a current account surplus for 1994 and 1995. Having trade deficit with their major trading partner, the EU, and having relatively low levels of current account surpluses, make these three countries also sensitive regarding their future ability to maintain the liberalization of trade with the EU in line with the EAA's expectations. Data on exports of commodities by SITC classification to the EU from CEE support the evidence of economic development differences among these countries. Latvia, Lithuania and partly Estonia have the largest value of their commodity exports to the EU in the SITC groups 2 and 3. Other countries with the EAA, including Slovenia, have the highest values of their exports in SITC commodity groups 6, 7 and 8. Only for Slovenia and Hungary is the biggest export value realized in group 7 (machinery, automotive products, etc.). Others have highest value in their exports in SITC groups 6 or 7 (semi-manufactured products and other consumer goods) (Appendix 1, Tables 1–10).

Foreign trade and current account developments of the CEE countries additionally support the previous observations. Adequate selection of the moment and type of enlargement is going to be influenced crucially by development differences among the CEE countries.

Beside the development achievements of the CEE countries and beside the possibilities of relatively fast economic development, the past enlargement experiences of the EU could be mentioned as arguments for the potential of the CEE countries to become full members.

In the past, the EU has often been enlarged with countries whose GDP was below the EU average. In the case of Spain and Portugal, for example, accession took place *just ten years after* both countries emerged from dictatorship. Their membership in the EU helped them towards faster growth. Their GDP has increased from 70% and 53% of the EU GDP average level by 7% and 16% points from their accession to this date.

The accession of the CEE countries will be based, at least in some cases, on an even greater difference between the average GDP value of the CEE countries and the EU. In terms of purchasing power parity the level of present GDP of countries like Poland, Hungary, the Czech Republic and Slovakia *is only around one third of the EU average*, while the GDP of Romania and

Bulgaria *is even lower, around one fifth of the EU average GDP*. The development gap measured in the relative level of GDP could be gradually closed as noted above. *The time necessary* for reaching the relative GDP level which was characteristic, for example, of Spain or Portugal at the moment of entry *depends on the economic growth differential* between the EU and accessing countries.

Production restructuring and in many cases promising development results of the CEE countries, together with development experiences of Asian Tigers, support the relevance of the assumption that at least some countries with the EAA, will be able to close development gap enough to catch up with the development requirements of the EU. The relative level of GDP which was acceptable in the cases of Spain and Portugal could well be implemented in the case of the CEE countries.

That way, a substantial potential for additional benefits the acceleration of development, due to the future effects of integration, will be constructed for old and new members of the EU. Going back to our train example, we can say that a number of running passengers from the CEE group have considerably good chances to jump on the accelerating EU integration train, provided that the EU is in fact determined to accept new members who are advanced enough to be able to compete adequately on the enlarged internal market of the EU. It is also obvious to everybody that the expected decision about the EU enlargement could not be based on the economic results of the CEE countries only. A great deal of the positive enlargement decision will be determined politically.

2.8   Potential Options for the EU Enlargement

Among the CEE countries and among members of the EU, potential scenarios of the EU enlargement are debated. It is not yet possible to estimate which of the enlargement recipes could get the majority support in both groups of countries. It is not possible, as will be clarified shortly, to prepare a convincing estimate of the economic (and political) consequences for each possible development option. Options discussed and potentially feasible (on certain assumptions) can be grouped into five models. Beside these models, which will be drawn up later, there are other eventual options which seem rather irrelevant, like immediate full membership of all CEE countries wishing to join EU, no new membership from the CEE group, the acceptance of the CEE countries one by one, etc.

Development differences among the CEE countries based on potentials for development gap closing, together with the ability of achieving relevant levels of economic and legal harmonization, suggest that a *gradual group EU membership model* could be implemented in the future. The CEE countries for example could be distributed into two groups (according to economic and harmonization criteria). The more advanced group could enter the EU relatively soon, the other group after some time. It is important for the successful realization of such an enlargement model that the requirements for both groups should be the same and that the EU provide guarantees for the second group, regarding their future membership.

Such a model has the advantage that membership criteria are specified and membership guarantees are given. There are some problems and difficulties attached to such a model. Not all countries in the group will fully meet the requirements at the same time. To make the model acceptable, it would be necessary to define membership requirements within specific ranges, to prevent better prepared potential members from having to wait for the less prepared. Beside problems of defining proper ranges for criteria there are some other difficulties connected to such an enlargement model. The competition between the CEE countries to satisfy EU requirements may lead to a substantial decrease in their willingness to develop intra-regional economic and political cooperation. On the other hand, increased competition could produce better results in the necessary development and harmonization areas. Grouping could also develop a negative reaction in the 'second' group of countries, especially in the areas of political attractiveness of implementing adjustments demanded by a 'relatively' remote EU membership. Grouping could lead to some decrease in the harmonization efforts of countries in the first group, feeling that they are more or less accepted as new members. Above all, the concept of gradual two group level membership could be politically difficult to be accepted even within the EU. Political reaction among the CEE countries to such an approach could be negative too, following the perception that 'CEE countries are really small fish for the EU', meaning that enlargement is not at all problematic for the EU. This idea is often combined with the suggestion that enlargement of the EU by CEE countries could follow the example of the enlargement with the former East Germany, where adjusting the economy came only after receiving full membership. It is obvious that such an attitude underestimates the costs of enlargement covered by one member of the EU: Germany. It is obvious that this enlargement model cannot satisfy all those who are convinced that rapid (practically immediate) membership in the EU is essential for securing the democratization process in the CEE countries.

The second model of enlargement could be the *gradual partial/full membership*, meaning that the CEE countries could be accepted into membership of the EU according to the fulfilment of the criteria for the different constituent parts (pillars) of the EU (economic, political, security). The eventual utilization of such a model would demand the entire redefinition of the EU membership. This process would be relatively complicated, touching on some internal EU problems and relations. If the redefinition of membership is possible, the sequence of gradual full membership could be:

security membership, internal market membership, political membership, full membership with parallel monetary union membership.

The model would probably be rejected not only among members of the EU, but among politicians from the CEE countries as well. In such model of enlargement the present requirements would be turned from the present function of 'integration tool' into an instrument of keeping some countries out of full membership for an unknown period of time.

The third model could be a combination of the above two models. It could be called the *gradual group partial membership model*.

The fourth model could be based on fulfilling the content of the EEA, without securing the full membership after the fulfilment of the Agreement's requirements. The *non-enlargement model* is not acceptable for the CEE countries. They understand that the EAA is just a necessary step to be taken before entering the full EU membership. The non-enlargement model could be feasible for a shorter period, especially if present members of the EU will be more inclined to 'deepen the integration'. Only after the successful implementation of the Monetary Union and after its stable performance could the dialogue start to accept new members. In such a scenario, serious discussion of enlargement could only be started probably a few years after the year 2000, and the actual enlargement could take another few years. In such a model, political discomfort on the side of the CEE countries will be strong, and the actual reactions would be difficult to assess. Most probably even within the EU not all members would support such a model. The chances for the model to be implemented depend rather substantially on the eventual change in the decision-making process, accepted as a result of the Inter-Governmental Conference (IGC), and the voting potential of individual EU members. That model makes the effective preparation for membership quite long (perhaps around ten years) and would probably lead to the decreased intensity of the harmonization efforts in the CEE countries. This model would result in relations based on a Free Trade Area between the two groups of countries. Preparation for engendered by a rather remote membership in the EU will develop less economic and legal convergence as other potential models of enlargement.

A fifth model could be based on similar concepts as are used to prepare EU member countries for their membership in the EMU. The *enlargement model based on criteria fulfilment* could be based on a list of necessary criteria to be fulfilled before membership and on an explicit time (may be with an early and a final option) when, if the criteria are fulfilled, CEE countries will definitely be able to enter the EU. The list of criteria could be more extensive than the list used for preparing for the EMU. On the other hand, it should not be too extensive, and it should contain criteria which are objectively measurable. Before implementing the list of criteria, as a tool for measuring the preparation level for membership, a necessary level of data accuracy and comparability should be assured. At present, as already mentioned, some official data do not reflect the actual performance of the CEE economies. For example, GDP in a number of CEE countries is probably underestimated due to the effects of the grey economy. Similar problems arise with measuring unemployment, sometimes inflation, etc. The selected criteria should follow the content of present requirements of the EAA and the 1995 White Paper, but at the same time they have to be easy to understand and interpret.

The levels of criteria (indicators) should be indicated in relative terms based on comparison with the relevant EU average data. The difference between the achievements of the CEE countries and the comparable EU data should be decided in advance: for example 50% of comparable EU data, etc. It could be decided whether the base of comparison in the EU averages should be at the moment when the criteria are established, or at the moment when the EU membership is going to be effective. The model could produce better results if a specific joint (EU-CEE) institution could be established to facilitate and supervise the process of preparing for the membership.

A list of the EU membership criteria could contain the following indicators:

- GDP and GDP per capita levels
- inflation rate
- budget deficit in % of GDP
- long-term interest rate
- unemployment rate
- competitiveness rate of selected industries
- current account and balance of payments deficit
- legislative approximation (accepted and implemented legal documents)
- etc.

The model in fact follows the spirit of the EAAs and the White Paper. The major difference is that it decides relative levels and lists of criteria to be fulfilled. It also sets explicitly a time for enlargement (possibly in two periods).

The model could help to clarify some misunderstanding concerning the present intentions of the EU regarding the use of provisions included in the EAAs and in the White Paper. It could help the governments of the CEE countries to follow more focused economic policies, together with strengthening the position of the governments when they suggest solutions that would hurt certain segments of their economies or societies. A more detailed elaboration of the idea behind the fifth possible model of enlargement could lead to a solution equally acceptable for the CEE countries and the EU.

For this model, the determination of the date of accession remains an open question. A short period until the first possible entry date (for example 1 January 2001), could be unacceptable for some CEE countries. The solution could not lie in moving that date forward, but in setting a second date two or three years ahead. It could also be considered whether the idea of two wave membership fits the model. As with a lot of other decisions regarding the enlargement, this question also depends a great deal on political considerations.

2.9   Preparing the CEE Countries for the Enlargement

There is no better solution for the CEE countries—in economic terms and most probably in the political and security areas as well—than to proceed with their harmonization efforts in order to filfil gradually the requirements of the integration with the EU.

The global trade liberalization process and an increasing number of economic integrations established around the world demand an adequate response from the CEE countries. Their membership in the World Trade Organisation (WTO) introduced a demand for rather extensive and relatively fast trade liberalization in goods and services towards all other members of the WTO. Their geographic location in Europe additionally exposes these countries to the strong economic and political impacts of the economic space created by the European Union, which expects to establish Monetary Union in 1999 at the latest.

Preparing for the membership in the EU on the part of the CEE countries' side is an extremely complex task given that they have to engage in a number of unavoidable policy measures which all have a strong effect on their development potential and generate substantial short-term adjustment costs.

These include:

- efforts for the gradual closing of the development gap with respect to the EU,
- trade liberalization measures required by the WTO's implementation of the Uruguay Round results,
- introduction of different forms of intra-regional cooperation based on numerous Free Trade Agreements concluded,
- adjusting their national legislation and their economic systems to a list of criteria determined by the pre-accession strategy of the EU.

That is the policies implemented to stimulate the convergence of development and to increase competitiveness and efficiency, the CEE countries will have to decide simultaneously on the dynamics and extent of the implementation of their bilateral or multilateral Free Trade Agreements (FTAs). The decision will be operationally influenced by unavoidable adjustments to global liberalization, expected to be most intensive in the coming years up to 2000. Global liberalization combined with regional FTAs produces decisive impacts on the CEE countries' preparation for the EU membership.

Whenever some 'classical' instruments had been put under the agreed common rules, individual states soon started to use other (new) regulatory measures. In such a way, classical import custom duties were replaced by quantitative restrictions and subsidies whenever it was possible.

After the Tokyo Round of the GATT negotiations, both instruments have been agreed to be used in specific circumstances only and in general were limited to the minimum. The response of international trade regulating practices of individual states was the introduction and use of new instruments like voluntary export restraints (VER), variable levies whenever they have been still allowed, specific customs procedures, etc.

After the Uruguay Round, that kind of 'new protection' practices have been further limited and gradually reduced in international trade of all goods and services. The process of trade liberalization in the scope of different FTAs has the same liberalization effect, but one in fact much broader.

It is obvious that the CEE countries' policies could not be immune to such tendencies. On the contrary, it could be expected that they are relatively more exposed to future temptations of introducing new protective techniques due to the accumulation of liberalization effects. They can also be exposed to such practices by third countries, because of their relatively less favourable position due to the agreed and implemented FTAs (Appendix 2, Table 2). Some of the new protection practices could be allowed on the basis of agreements (including the EAA), but past global experience suggests a possible escalation. It is important to stress that the competitive position on home markets in fact tends to deteriorate with respect to insiders to the agreement.

Changes in the competitive position on the domestic market can potentially mean that even the trade with the EU partners could be hindered by indirect restrictive practices. The reaction of outsiders to FTA or the European Agreements could be similarly based on the fact that their competitive position on the market of the insider country deteriorates vis-à-vis other insiders. This reasoning about the general influence of the FTAs gives additional support to the suggestion that the CEE countries should further prepare themselves for more effective competition on national and international markets.

The only characteristic of the potential revival of protectionist behaviour common to all three levels is that the country introducing such practice will do it mostly by means of policy instruments of internal economic regulation.

It is becoming more and more important to implement an effective monitoring of potential digressions from agreed rules of liberalization, especially in the cases of FTAs and also in the case of implementing the European Association Agreements. The CEE countries should develop and implement methods for monitoring the effects of market opening and of all other impacts on the economy brought forward by the process of the pre-accession activity. Proper monitoring of integration effects, together with the collection of relevant data, one of the necessary preconditions for the proper and effective utilization of the safeguard mechanisms incorporated into the Agreements.

It is vital for the successful integration, be it of the FTA or EAA type, that the removal of classical barriers to economic cooperation is not neutralized by the introduction of any 'new' barriers, including, for example, a public procurement policy of individual governments. The potential dangers of negative integration practices threatens both the EU and CEE.

Indicators of the effects of integration on economic development are obviously numerous and diverse (Balassa, 1974; Classens, 1992). They are not always reliable enough, especially when they are used ex ante, for the assessment of dynamic effects. The problem is clearly evident when, for example, an evaluation of the 1995 White Paper is performed by the CEE countries or by the EU representatives. The absence of strong and convincing evidence about the effects of the implementation of the White Paper could lead to the following extreme attitudes with respect to its role in the accession process.

The White Paper is, according to its substance, a guideline which has to be applied in full before the CEE countries could enter the EU. Concerning the White Paper, the discussion between the EU and the CEE countries could be limited to only two questions: when can membership take place and how could membership be achieved.

The official representatives of the EU are convinced that the content of the White Paper is the necessary minimum to secure effective and productive enlargement of the EU. Some officials from the EU (on the basis of other assumptions, which could also not be based on solid analytical evidence) show a different attitude to the role of the White Paper. They suggest that during the process of accession it will be decided which demands of the White Paper are really essential and necessary to be fulfilled before entering the EU. Their attitude is based on the assumption that it is up to the individual countries to decide what is possible and necessary to adopt from the White Paper, based on its development position, since the document is a recommendation. Such a position regarding the role of White Paper is rather liberal, but in fact it is even more confusing for the acceding countries.

There is a third understanding of the role of the White Paper which further complicates the preparation of the enlargement process. The requirements are proper and correct regarding the future effective functioning of the enlarged Union. Nevertheless, they could be realized gradually, faster and more effectively after actually entering the EU. Such views are advocated by politicians and even by some professional economists from the CEE countries. Eventual disputes related to this position could only be relatively subjective due to the scarcity of the relevant data regarding the future development effects on the CEE countries and present EU members.

Integrating into the internal market is a much more complex effort than the formation of the FTA. In fact, the content of the EAA suggests directly only the creation of the FTA. Numerous concepts contained in the EAA indirectly suggest that integration will exceed the bare content of an FTA. Parts of the EAA relating to market competition rules, standardization, legal harmonization, statistical cooperation, etc., openly indicate that the Agreement is meant to exceed the content of a 'clasical' free trade agreement. It means that EAA in fact already present a conceptual framework for internal market development. The White Paper gives only the operational description of the activities necessary to undertake in order to join the internal market. Beside trade liberalization issues, internal market integration requires harmonization of rules, policies and national laws. This is often explained as a process of a gradual adoption of the 'acquis communautaire' by the CEE countries wishing to be accepted as new members of the EU. The vital guidelines are evidently contained in the 1995 White Paper. The complexity of the document and the enormity of the needed legislative adjustments will assure the spending of a considerable amount of energy and time. It is most probably necessary for the CEE countries to follow those guidelines if they wish to participate effectively in the highly demanding form of integration characteristic to the internal market type. Those CEE countries who will not be able or willing to follow the suggested adjustments, will probably have the option to be connected to the EU by a lower level of integration type, for example just by an FTA.

According to the Essen accession criteria, intra-European and intra-regional cooperation, through the establishment of economic, trade and physical links (transport, energy, telecommunications included), is an essential part of the pre-accession strategy. This of course refers to links not only between individual members of the CEE group and the EU, but equally importantly between the CEE countries themselves. Supposing that in many instances the level of economic convergence among the CEE countries is higher than in relation to the EU, the development effects from the intra-regional CEE integration (FTAs) could be rather promising. Preparing for the accession from the point of view of economic theory (Appendix 2, Table 2) and based on practical evidences, suggests without doubt that the CEE countries should support intra-regional cooperation in order to increase the general level of their convergence with the EU.

The preparation of the CEE countries for enlargement could be more focused and much more efficient if a more elaborate idea of the fifth enlargement model could be implemented in practice. The elaboration of the model could eliminate all concerns about the role of the White Paper and of the potential extenuation of accession criteria. We can hope that answers to the 'Questionnaire', provided by the CEE countries, have established the necessary information for a fast, reasonable and concrete preparation of the list of relative criteria for membership in the EU, as is being suggested in the fifth potential enlargement model.

2.10 Summary

It is not possible to decide purely on economic grounds when and what type of integration could be implemented between the EU and CEE. Full membership of CEE in the future EU is favoured without exceptions by the members of the CEE group. They wish to have it realized as soon as possible. Beside economic reasons, an important role will be played by internal and external political considerations when the EU will deliberate on the issue of enlargement.

Future membership of the CEE countries in the EU is possible and acceptable only if it can secure to old and to new members long-term positive economic, social and security achievements. Such overall positive achievements could be in fact realized, according to international trade theory and according to practical experiences, only when the necessary level of economic and political convergence among integration partners is fulfilled.

In six months, after the end of the IGC work, it is expected that negotiations for full membership in the EU will be started with all CEE countries. It is not possible to predict how the negotiations will proceed. Most probably, two elements will characterise the negotiations: the development level of associated countries and the model of enlargement selected by the EU. It is reasonable to doubt that the EU does not have a substantial economic and political interest in enlarging with members from the CEE group. One of the reasons for the EU's interests in the enlargement is the growing globalization of the world economy, with increasing world-wide competition characterized by an increased role of modern technological developments, bringing about a need for large open markets. The EU's interest in enlargement is strong, due to similar integration efforts present in other regions of the world. Beside economic interests, the EU has a strong political and security interest in enlargement. An integrated Europe in the economic and political sense could become a more stable and secure area.

The interest of the CEE countries in enlargement are similar to those of the EU, often further strengthened by the hopes to get additional support for faster economic development on the basis of full EU membership. It is often said that only fast full membership in the EU could secure economic development and the strengthening of the young democratic systems of those countries. The majority of the CEE countries are well aware of the fact that a major part of the effort to adjust and harmonize with the members of the present EU should be provided by them. Nevertheless, they appreciate and even need assistance from the EU in the form of different programs of financial support. It could be helpful for the further preparation for the EU membership if after the IGC, and on the basis of the answers to the Questionnaire, an analytical overview and a list of the necessary criteria for the membership could be elaborated.

Appendix 1   Commodity Structure of Foreign Trade Between the CEE Countries and the EU for 1994

Classification of products at SITC Nomenclature:

1 Beverages and tobacco
2 Crude materials, excl. fuels
3 Fuels and minerals
4 Animal, vegetable oil, fat
5 Chemicals
6 Basic manufactures
7 Machines, transport equipment
8 Miscellaneous manufactured goods
9 Goods not classified by kind

Table 1   Commodity (SITC) structure of exports and imports to the EU from Slovenia (1994)

in 1000 ECU	Import	Export	Balance
0	58834	195629	136795
1	6302	48914	41712
2	84655	123909	39254
3	118	74321	74203
4	1824	5900	4076
5	135411	395388	259977
6	989031	863323	−125708
7	1156709	1455513	298804
8	95436	440177	−516259
9	20316	12113	−8203

Source: Come, Intra- and Extra-EU trade, Eurostat, Luxembourg, 1995

Table 2   Commodity (SITC) structure of exports and imports to the EU from Hungary (1994)

in 1000 ECU	Import	Export	Balance
0	631718	350600	−281118
1	28618	30216	1598
2	310606	125155	−185451
3	58338	35420	−22918
4	8872	9376	504
5	389342	780828	391486
6	848571	1263211	414640
7	1417383	2539870	1122487
8	1161182	887448	−273734
9	47720	20927	−26793

Source: Come, Intra- and Extra-EU trade, Eurostat, Luxembourg, 1995

Table 3 Commodity (SITC) structure of exports and imports to the EU from Czech Republic (1994)

in 1000 ECU	Import	Export	Balance
0	195568	442805	247237
1	31538	62161	30623
2	449972	150829	−299143
3	182033	65303	−116730
4	7831	292205	21374
5	512970	886676	373706
6	1952534	1454997	−497537
7	1630968	3507769	1876801
8	1247784	1145970	−101814
9	112238	59190	−53048

Source: Come, Intra- and Extra-EU trade, Eurostat, Luxembourg, 1995

Table 4 Commodity (SITC) structure of exports and imports to the EU from Slovakia (1994)

in 1000 ECU	Import	Export	Balance
0	42894	108261	65367
1	304	11297	10993
2	92819	37976	−54843
3	7302	8683	1381
4	1996	1961	−35
5	160252	209239	48987
6	749780	379153	−370627
7	393293	795565	402272
8	399240	192855	−206385
9	13266	6699	−6567

Source: Come, Intra- and Extra-EU trade, Eurostat, Luxembourg, 1995

Table 5 Commodity (SITC) structure of exports and imports to the EU from Poland (1994)

in 1000 ECU	Import	Export	Balance
0	803840	870657	66817
1	8183	55065	46882
2	496575	254120	−242455
3	711160	199074	−512086
4	8921	83954	75033
5	433566	1569358	1135792
6	2603730	2467336	−136394
7	1509674	3772059	2262385
8	2403453	1238937	−1164516
9	73777	59049	−14728

Source: Come, Intra- and Extra-EU trade, Eurostat, Luxembourg, 1995

Table 6   Commodity (SITC) structure of exports and imports to the EU from
Romania (1994)

in 1000 ECU	Import	Export	Balance
0	76569	146749	70180
1	9457	19734	10277
2	69675	52044	–17631
3	75034	66670	–8364
4	5318	4210	–1108
5	128827	219000	90173
6	582066	733913	151847
7	216476	952251	735775
8	1313479	375514	–937965
9	12722	34887	22165

Source: Come, Intra- and Extra-EU trade, Eurostat, Luxembourg, 1995

Table 7   Commodity (SITC) structure of exports and imports to the EU from
Bulgaria (1994)

in 1000 ECU	Import	Export	Balance
0	116750	158683	41933
1	60621	58011	–2610
2	115048	51989	–63059
3	22085	56674	34589
4	2647	5886	3239
5	145307	264629	119322
6	404479	287739	–116740
7	162011	543383	381372
8	305802	213931	–91871
9	7032	8719	1687

Source: Come, Intra- and Extra-EU trade, Eurostat, Luxembourg, 1995

Table 8   Commodity (SITC) structure of exports and imports to the EU from Latvia
(1994)

in 1000 ECU	Import	Export	Balance
0	9148	65084	55936
1	342	52132	51790
2	161423	6012	–155411
3	314246	9740	–304506
4	8	6019	6011
5	23981	39623	12942
6	126349	54792	–71557
7	11694	167654	155960
8	64050	70172	6122
9	7362	13057	5696

Source: Come, Intra- and Extra-EU trade, Eurostat, Luxembourg, 1995

Table 9   Commodity (SITC) structure of exports and imports to the EU from
Estonia (1994)

in 1000 ECU	Import	Export	Balance
0	16518	61639	45121
1	180	15652	15472
2	65183	4392	–60791
3	35559	4440	–31119
4	41	6287	6246
5	30606	28894	–1712
6	68358	33819	–34539
7	5228	105931	100703
8	39415	34513	–4002
9	4069	5151	1082

Source: Come, Intra- and Extra-EU trade, Eurostat, Luxembourg, 1995

Table 10   Commodity (SITC) structure of exports and imports to the EU from
Lithuania (1994)

in 1000 ECU	Import	Export	Balance
0	29252	70133	40892
1	190	83078	82888
2	129893	11333	–118560
3	257673	3552	–254121
4	45	7631	7586
5	78352	72294	–6058
6	103903	92655	–11248
7	26253	263322	237069
8	100645	94851	–5794
9	4425	13696	10271

Source: Come, Intra- and Extra-EU trade, Eurostat, Luxembourg, 1995

Appendix 2   Wages in the CEE Countries, Change of Competitive Position

Table 1   Gross monthly wages in US$
(gross of income tax/net* of social security tax)

	1993	1994
Bulgaria	115	86
Czech R.	200	240
Hungary	296	317
Poland	221	241
Slovak R.	175	196
Slovenia*	414467	(602**)

** Monthly wages for 1995.

Source: East European monitor, January 1996, vol. 3. No. 1, p. 6 and
Monthly Bulletin, bank of Slovenia, March 1996, Table 3.8.

Table 2   Changes in the relative competitive position of insiders and outsiders
following implementation of FTA

		Target Market		
		A	B	C
	B	–	+	0
A's position	C	–	0	+
Relative to:	R	(–)	+	+
	A	(+)	–	–
R's position	B	–	–	
Relative to:	C	–	–	(+)

A, B, C are countries insiders to FTA and R is outsider country. Upper half of Table 2 summarizes the changes in the competitive position of A relative to other insiders (B, C) and to outsider (R). The lower half of Table shows the change in the competitive position of R on the FTA members markets.

+: improvement of competitive position,
–: deterioration of competitive position,
0: no change in competitive position.

Appendix 3 Some Potential Integration Effects

Table 1 Cost of EU's CEE Enlargement in 2000

	Countries		EU Budget Expenditures					EU Budget Receipts		Net payment (net receipt)	Net payment (net receipt)
			CAP	Structural P.	Others	Total	Total	Total	Total		
			Mil. ECU	Mil. ECU	Mil. ECU	Mil. ECU	% of GDP	Mil. ECU	% of GDP	Mil. ECU	% of GDP
1	Belgium	BE	1075	510	2838	4423	1.90	3676	1.58	747	0.32
2	Denmark	DK	1720	170	367	2257	1.48	1834	1.20	423	0.28
3	Germany	DE	6019	3401	4997	14417	0.67	27184	1.27	-12767	-0.60
4	Greece	EL	4300	3740	144	8183	11.50	1281	1.80	6902	9.70
5	Spain	ES	4730	6120	1083	11933	2.23	6435	1.20	5498	1.03
6	France	FR	9460	2379	2839	14678	1.10	17130	1.28	-2452	-0.18
7	Ireland	IE	1720	3204	121	5045	8.41	1139	1.90	3906	6.51
8	Italy	IT	3053	4726	2175	9953	0.96	11880	1.15	-1927	-0.19
9	Luxembourg	LU	22	34	955	1011	7.15	212	1.50	799	5.65
10	Netherlands	NL	2580	170	768	3518	1.05	5539	1.65	-2021	-0.60
11	Portugal	PT	1290	5780	194	7264	7.59	1483	1.55	5781	6.04
12	Great Britain	GB	4456	2720	2282	9459	0.91	12488	1.20	-3029	-0.29
13	Austria	AT	1004	401	401	1806	0.90	2569	1.28	-763	-0.38
14	Finland	FI	1003	358	236	1597	1.36	1508	1.28	89	0.08
15	Sweden	SE	566	287	378	1230	0.65	2417	1.28	-1187	-0.63
	EU-15		42997	34000	19778	96775	1.28	96775	1.28	0	0.00
	% of total		44.4	35.10	20.50	100.00					
	Estimates (Incl. Structural change, CAP reform, Uruguay Round) of the Cost of CEE Countries' EU Membership										
16	Belgaria	BU	417	835	33	1285	10.23	161	1.28	1124	8.95
17	Czech Rep.	CS	904	1625	136	2664	5.10	669	1.28	1996	3.82
18	Hungary	HU	2166	2848	150	5165	8.94	739	1.28	4425	7.66
19	Poland	PO	3290	6480	327	10097	8.04	1608	1.28	8490	6.76
20	Romania	RO	3957	6163	104	10223	25.68	510	1.28	9714	24.40
21	Slovakia	SV	396	1705	46	2147	12.21	225	1.28	1921	10.93
	CEE 6		11130	19656	794	31581	10.34	3911	1.28	27670	9.06
22	Slovenia	SL	313	648	50	1011	5.23	248	1.28	764	3.95
23	Estonia	EO	198	351	17	566	8.44	86	1.28	480	7.16
24	Latvia	LA	260	423	20	703	9.21	98	1.28	605	7.93
25	Lithuania	LI	299	541	20	859	11.36	97	1.28	762	10.08
	CEE 10		12200	21618	902	34720	10.01	4439	1.28	30281	8.73

Net receipt of CEE 6 in % of EU-GDP (EU Budget) 0.37 28.59

Net receipt of CEE 10 in % of EU-GDP (EU Budget) 0.40 31.29

Source: Breuss (1996)

Table 2   Maastricht Convergence Criteria: (EU 1995 and 1997) and CEE Countries (1995) (Article 109; EC Treaty)

	Price stability Inflation rate[1] (in %)			General government Deficit[2] (% of GDP)			General government Gross Debt[2] (% of GDP)			Long-term nominal interest rates (in %)			Exchange rates in EMS		Fulfilled all criteria	
													within 'normal' bands	ERM participation	exact interpretation	mild interpretation[3]
	1995	1996	1997	1995	1996	1997	1995	1996	1997	1995	1996	1997	1995	1995	1997	1997
Belgium	1.5	2.4	2.2	-4.5	-3.1	-3.5	134.4	132.3	130.0	7.6	6.8	6.8	yes	yes	no	yes
Denmark	2.0	2.4	2.7	-2.0	-1.3	-0.5	73.6	72.7	70.5	8.3	7.5	7.5	yes	yes	no	yes[3]
Germany	1.8	2.1	2.2	-3.5	-3.5	-3.0	61.0	62.0	61.0	6.9	6.3	6.3	yes	yes	no	yes
Greece	9.2	7.9	7.0	-9.3	-8.3	-7.3	144.4	114.0	113.1	18.4	18.0	18.0	no	no	no	no
Spain	4.9	3.9	3.6	-5.9	-4.7	-3.6	64.8	65.8	65.4	10.9	9.8	9.7	no	yes	yes	no
France	1.9	2.1	1.8	-5.0	-3.9	-2.9	51.5	53.4	54.2	7.6	6.9	6.8	yes	yes	no	yes
Ireland	2.5	2.3	2.4	-2.7	-2.0	-1.3	85.9	81.3	76.9	8.3	7.7	7.7	yes	yes	no	yes
Italy	5.6	4.3	3.7	-7.4	-6.0	-5.2	124.9	123.9	122.3	11.8	10.8	10.4	no	no	no	no
Luxembourg	1.9	2.2	2.5	0.4	0.6	0.7	6.3	6.7	6.8	6.2	6.0	6.0	yes	yes	yes	yes
Netherlands	1.6	1.8	2.0	-3.1	-2.7	-2.2	78.4	78.2	77.8	7.0	6.3	6.3	no	no	no	yes
Austria	2.4	2.3	2.4	-6.1	-4.5	-3.0	68.0	71.0	70.0	6.7	6.6	6.6	yes	yes	no	yes
Portugal	4.2	3.6	3.3	-5.4	-4.7	-4.1	70.5	71.0	70.9	11.7	11.0	11.0	yes	yes	no	yes
Finland	1.2	2.0	2.2	-5.4	-1.5	0.0	63.2	64.4	64.5	8.0	7.3	7.3	yes	no	no	no
Sweden	2.8	2.6	3.0	-7.0	-4.5	-3.2	81.4	80.8	79.8	10.3	8.8	8.8	no	no	no	yes
Great Britain	2.9	3.0	2.6	-5.1	-3.7	-2.8	52.2	53.3	53.2	8.2	7.9	7.9	no	no	no	yes[3]
EU-15 average	3.1	3.0	2.7	-4.8	-3.6	-2.8	71.0	71.6	71.3	9.2	8.5	8.5			Countries	Countries
Reference values	2.9	3.5	3.5	-3.0	-3.0	-3.0	60.0	60.0	60.0	9.5	8.6	8.5			2	9(11)
Poland	25			-3.1			63.5			29.0						
Hungary	28			-3.5			–			34.0						
Czech R.	9			0.0			13.1			12.9						
Slovak R.	12			-4.7			–			9.8						
Romania	29			-3.3			–			51.0						
Bulgaria	80			-6.0			83.1			34.0						
Lithuania	25			-2.0			–			18.5						
Latvia	20			-2.0			–			15.9						
Estonia	30			-4.1			17.9									
Slovenia	8.6			0.0			–									

[1] Treaty on European Union (TEU, Protocol 6): price stability is measured by the consumer prices index. The forecasts by the European Commission and by the OECD use instead the private consumption deflator.

[2] EC Treaty, Article 104c (2) and Protocol 5 TEU; [3] Denmark and Great Britain have 'opted out' from EMU (Protocols 11 and 12 TEU).

EMS = European Monetary System; ERM = Exchange Rate Mechanism of the EMS.

Source: Breuss (1996), Poročevalec, no. 8, 1996, Ljubljana other sources

Table 3 The Impact of EU Membership of the CEEs example of Austria in 2008

	4 CEEs[1]		Poland	5 other CEEs[2]	10 CEEs
	Direct effects[3]	Total effects[4]	Total effects[4]		
	(Cumulative percentage deviations from the baseline scenario (association status) over the period 2000 to 2008)				
Gross Domestic Product (GDP), real	+0,8	+1,5	+0,1	+0,1	+1,7
Gross fixed capital formation, real	+1,5	+2,9	+0,2	+0,1	+3,2
Private consumption, real	+0,6	+1,1	+0,1	+0,1	+1,4
Exports of goods and services, real	+1,7	+2,9	+0,2	+0,1	+3,2
Imports of goods and services, real	+1,7	+2,9	+0,2	+0,2	+3,3
Private consumption deflator	–0,1	–0,1	+0,0	+0,0	–0,1
Real disposable income of households	+0,8	+1,4	+0,1	+0,1	+1,7
Dependent employment (% change) (in 1.000)	+0,5 +16,8	+0,9 +30,2	+0,1 +2,2	+0,1 +1,9	+1,1 +34,3
Unemployment rate (change)	–0,2	–0,4	–0,0	–0,0	–0,4
General government financial balance (% of GDP, change)[5] (bil)	+0,3 +12,1	+0,5 +19,4	–0,0 –1,1	–0,1 –3,9	+0,4 +14,4

CEEs = Central and Eastern European countries.

[1] Czech Republic, Hungary, Slovakia, Slovenia.

[2] Bulgaria, Estonia, Latvia, Lithuania, Rumania.

[3] Direct trade creation effects.

[4] Direct trade creation effects plus indirect trade effects via GDP stimulation in the EU and trade creation through transfer payments to the CEEs.

[5] Net lending of general government (+ = improvement, – is deterioration).

Source: Breuss (1996).

Table 4 Integration Quality in the EAA versus EU-Membership (Topics in the Negotiations for Accession)

		Applicable on the EAA bases	Applicable only after EU-Membership
1	Free movement of goods (elimination of border controls)	no	yes
2	Free movement of services and freedom of settlement	yes	yes
3	Free movement of persons	no	yes
4	Free movement of capital	no	yes
5	Traffic policy (transit problem)	yes(no)	yes(new)
6	Common competition policy	no	yes
7	Common consumers safeguard and health protection	no(yes)	yes
8	Reseach and information technology	no(yes)	yes
9	Education (general and professional)	partly, yes	yes
10	Statistics	–	–
1	Company law	no	yes
2	Social policy (social chart)	no	yes
3	Environment	no	yes
4	Energy	no	yes
5	Agriculture (CAP)	no	yes
6	Fishery	no	yes
7	Customs union	no	yes
8	Trade relations	no	yes
9	Structural instruments (also ECSC)	no	yes
10	Regional policy	no	yes
1	Industrial policy	no	yes
2	Tax policy	no	yes
3	Economic and monetary policy (EMU)	no	yes
4	Foreign and security policy (CFSP)	no	yes
5	Justice and home affairs (CJHA)	no	yes
6	Other rules of the TEU	no	yes
7	Finance and budgetary rules	no	yes
8	Institutions	no	yes
9	Others	no	yes

CAP = Common Agricultural Policy;
CFSP = Common Foreign and Security Policy;
EAA = European Association Agreement;
EU = Europoean Union;
ECSC = European Coal and Steel Community;
EMU = European Monetary Union;
CJHA = Cooperation in Justice and Home Affairs;
TEU = Treaty on European Union (Maastricht treaty).

References

Agreement on Government Procurement (1988): GATT: Geneva (revised text).

Balassa, Bela (1974): 'Trade Creation and Trade Diversion in the European Common Market: An Appraisal of the Evidence', The Manchester School of Economic and Social Studies 42, 2:93–135.

Baldwin, Richard E. (1993): 'The Potential for Trade Between the Countries of EFTA and Central and East Europe', EFTA Occasional Paper No. 44.

Baldwin, Richard E. (1994): 'Towards an Integrated Europe', CEPR.

Barro Robert-Xavier Sala-I-Martin (1991): 'Convergence Across States and Regions', Brooking Papers on Economic Activity, 1.

Baumol, William J. (1986): 'Productivity Growth, Convergence and Welfare: What the Long Run Data Show', American Economic Review 76, 5:1072–1085.

Bruess F. (1996): 'Austria's Approach Towards the EU', paper presented at the expert meeting on 'The Economic Aspects of Slovenia's Integration into the European Union', Bled, 12–13 April 1996, organised by the Trans-European Policy Studies Association (TEPSA) and Center for International Relations, University Ljubljana.

Cilj, E. S. (1993): 'Slovenija in notranji evropski trg', Snoj.D. (ed.) Gospodarski vestnik, Ljubljana.

Classens E. (1992): 'Measuring European Integration across Partners and Industries'; An Application of the 'Monnet Index', Commission of the EU.

Eurobarometer-Central and Eastern, Public Opinion and the European Union (1996), No. 6, European Commission, Brussels.

European Economy: Reports and Studies (1994): 'The Economic Interpenetration between the European Union and Eastern Europe', No. 6., Directorate General, European Commission, Brussels.

East Europe Monitor, ISSN 1353-4696, published by Business Monitor International Ltd.

Findlay, Robert (1987): 'Comparative Advantage', in: J. Eatwell-M. Milgate-P. Newman (eds.) The New Palgrave: A Dictionary of Economics, vol. 1, Macmillan: London.

Ekins, P. (n. d.): Trading of the Future: The New Economic Foundations, London.

Inotai Andras (n. d.): 'The System of Criteria for Hungary's Accession to the European Union', Trends in World Economy, No. 76, Institute of World Economics, Budapest.

Inotai Andras (1995): 'From Association Agreements to Full Membership? The Dynamics of Relations between the Central and Eastern European Countries and the EU', Institute for World Economics, Budapest.

Kawecka-Wyrzykowska, Elzbieta (1996): 'Cost and Benefits of the Eastward Enlargement of the EU: Selected Issues', Foreign Trade Institute, Warsaw (draft).

Krugman, Paul R. (1990): 'Rethinking International Trade', MIT Press: Cambridge MA.

Kumar Andrej (1994): 'Regional Trade in Central Europe—Slovenian Perspective', RBMP, Bled, Slovenia.

Lucas Robert E. Jr. (1988): 'On the Mechanics of Economic Development', Journal of Monetary Economics 22, 3–42.

Monthly Bulletin (1996): Bank of Slovenia, Ljubljana.

Regionalism and the World Trading System (1995), World Trade Organisation, Geneva.

Rosati David (1995): 'Impediments to Poland's Accession to the European Union: Real or Imaginary?', in: E.Kawecka-Wyrzykowska-T.Roe (eds.) Polish Agriculture and Enlargement of the European Union, Warsaw School of Economics.

Solow, Robert M. (1973): 'Growth Theory', in: D.Greenaway-M.Beaney-I.M.T. Steward (eds.). Companion to Contemporary Economic Thought, Routledge: London, pp. 393–415.

The Potential for Trade Growth in the New Europe (1993), EFTA Bulletin, 4.

White Paper (1995): Preparation of the Associated Countries of Central and Eastern Europe for Integration into the Internal Market of the EU, presented by the Commission, COM(95) 163 final, Brussels.

3

On the Benefits of the Accession for Western and Eastern Europe

Elżbieta Kawecka-Wyrzykowska
Foreign Trade Institute, Warsaw

3.1   Introduction[1]

The broad goal of integrating the Central and East European (CEE) countries[2] into the European Union seems to be widely shared in the EU. In its Copenhagen Declaration of June 1993 the EU offered membership of the Union to those former CMEA countries that wished to join and fulfilled certain political and economic criteria. The Associated Countries have often strongly expressed their desire for membership in the Union. No decision, however, has been taken so far by the Union on the time-table of negotiations or on the required, clearly defined, conditions. Meanwhile, arguments that enlargement will be very costly for the EU persist. Behind the concern lies the possibility that the EU wants to postpone difficult decisions.

We argue here that:

(i)   Eastward enlargement will be beneficial to all partners.
(ii) Postponing the decision on the accession of CEE countries is risky and may harm the whole European continent.

3.2   The CEE Countries' Motives for Achieving Membership of the EU

There are three sets of reasons why the CEE countries wish to attain EU membership: economic, political and systemic.

Economic benefits resulting from unrestricted access to a larger market are well known to economists. They involve various manifestations of economies of scale, better allocation of resources, elimination of distortions in production, unconstrained flow of productive resources to the most efficient uses, and as a result of all this, an increase in GDP.

One could say that the CEE countries have already benefited from most of these elements as a result of the free trade area being set up under the Europe Agreements. This is particularly the case for those countries which were first to sign the agreements. Establishment of the free trade area will be completed in the next few years. What we see here, however, is only part of the picture.

First, provisions in the free trade area do not cover agricultural products; liberalization in this area is very limited and selective.[3] Most CEE countries have a comparative advantage in agricultural products. Depriving these countries of easy access to the EU market and allowing Western economies free access to CEE industrial markets when the EU has a clear comparative advantage in industrial products raises doubts about CEE gains in these areas. Second, even when all border barriers are removed, other obstacles—physical, technical, administrative, etc.—will remain. These obstacles are linked to different systems, different regulations, different currencies (transaction costs), differences in required norms and standards (lack of harmonization), etc. They are very similar to obstacles EU producers faced before completion of the single European market. The elimination of certain 'formalities' in cross-border trade would reduce substantially transaction costs and increase the CEE countries' export opportunities.

The possible benefits from an increase in EU integration were estimated in the famous Cecchini report to amount to a rise of several percentage points in GDP levels. The CEE countries should achieve similar benefits from joining the internal European market. It could be argued that in the case of the CEE countries the advantages will be even greater because of larger differences in economic development at the point of departure. In other words, 'many of the economic arguments which justified the completion of the Community's internal market in the 1980s apply in just the same way to the enlargement of the Union' (Mayhew 1996, p. 36).

It is true also that CEE countries are interested in financial support from the EU budget (access to various funds, including structural funds). As member states they would be eligible for some funds which might be used to modernize their economies, reduce sensitive regional problems, etc. The significance of this factor should not be overestimated, however.

There are other economic benefits. These are related, for instance, to the free movement of workers, which is one of the four pillars of the EU's internal market. The CEE countries are aware of the fact that this is one of the most sensitive issues in the debate on accession and that they will have to accept a transition period in this area of mutual cooperation with the EU. They would not like, however, to be deprived of the benefits resulting from this 'freedom'.

Modernization of the CEE economies is a condition for their sustained growth. Such modernization is, however, not possible without a large inflow of foreign direct investments (Inotai, 1993). Some sectors are still underdeveloped, including many service industries. Their potential development raises prospects not only for CEE consumers but also for foreign investors who can expand their activities and increase profits. All in all, greater integration would act as a way to multiply benefits, creating new opportunities for cooperation in several other areas.

While economic benefits are important, there are other positive aspects of an eastward enlargement of the EU. Political and security motives for enlargement undoubtedly play a big, or even bigger role, than purely economic considerations. There is a fear that the Central and Eastern Europe countries, on their own, might become vulnerable to their Russian neighbour. Poland in particular feels insecure. The CEE countries, which are predominantly small, would have better chances for cooperation as partners within the framework of a wider agreement of multilateral character.[4] There is also a desire for the West to recognize that the CEE countries belong to Europe, and share a similar heritage and common values.

The third benefit of EU membership is linked to the expected positive effects on the stabilization of policy-making in the CEE countries.[5] This would be the same as the political and economic stabilizing role the EU played at the time of its southward expansion. Admission of the CEE countries into the EU would introduce more discipline into domestic policies. It would also make a significant contribution towards the consolidation of reforms in those countries and strengthening the confidence of the general public and investors. Admission would anchor the CEE countries in market economies and in democratic political institutions. Other effects would be to increase the credibility of Poland and other CEE countries and, from the foreign investor's point of view, reduce the uncertainty of doing business in those countries.

Yet another effect of membership would be to reduce the EU's enactment of anti-dumping legislation and other protectionist measures. Such measures have been recently applied by the EU against products in which CEE countries have their greatest export opportunities. Such measures have threatened not only exports of goods from the CEE countries but also foreign direct investments in those countries. Foreign investors fear that after establishing a company in a Central European country, their products exported to the EU may also face accusations of unfair practices and risk contingent protection measures. Free trade areas that have been in the process of creation under the Europe Agreements have not eliminated neither reduced the possibility of applying these acts of protection. Thus, membership in the EU would engender more secure expectations for foreign investors in the new market economies of Central and Eastern Europe, eliminating one of the main obstacles to expansion of foreign direct investments.

The same positive effects would follow adjustments to or the modelling of the CEE countries' domestic systems on those in the EU, for example, capital markets and banking systems (Buch, 1995).

All in all, EU membership would strengthen CEE countries' security, consolidate the process of democratic changes, enhance the progress of economic transformation, and contribute to sustained growth. Discussion of the implications of EU membership should not, however, neglect the potential costs for the CEE countries. These could be on a political level—for example, in the form of reduced autonomy in carrying out economic and social policies, or applying legal mechanisms—or economic—that is, through increased competition for CEE producers. Most of the costs in question, however, are those involving the transformation of their less developed economies, rather than those related to integration. Each country should also consider the cost of not joining the EU.

3.3   EU Benefits from Eastward Enlargement

The strengthening of economic and political ties with Central and Eastern Europe is also in the interest of the European Union. Many of the benefits resulting from the enlargement are similar to those expected to accrue to the CEE countries.

Security is a common interest of all European countries. In particular, the EU is viewed as an anchor of stability for Europe as a whole. It has an interest not only in preserving its internal stability but also in preserving peace in Europe. Leaving the CEE countries in a 'grey area' between the politically stable West and the still volatile political situation in the East, would leave a large, insecure area around the Eastern borders of the Union. Lack of security in Europe would harm the whole process of integration.

The EU has also an obvious interest in the trading opportunities offered by the new market economies in Central and Eastern Europe. Accession of the CEE countries to the EU would allow trade to expand, thus benefiting West European production and jobs. Expansion of trade would bring a number of advantages to both the CEE countries and the EU, some of which have been already mentioned above. It would also increase the competitiveness of the EU on an international scale, for example, as a result of cheaper supplies of some resources and enhanced economies of scale. Thus, the Eastward enlargement is a way to ensure Europe's role in global politics and in the global world economy to the benefit of both the EU and CEE countries.

It must be remembered that over the past several years, EU countries benefited much from increased trade with Central and Eastern Europe. EU imports increased more slowly than EU exports to CEE, although industrial imports had not yet taken advantage of liberalization measures undertaken in most CEE countries by the beginning of 1995. As a result, the EU's trade deficit, which amounted to ECU 5.5 billion in 1989 (in trade with Poland, the Czech Republic, Slovakia, Hungary, Romania and Bulgaria) was transformed into trade surpluses of ECU 5.5 billion in 1993, ECU 4.6 billion in 1994 and ECU 5.4 billion in 1995.[6] In the CEE countries, the prevailing opinion is that the formal asymmetry, which was to their benefit, has turned into actual asymmetry in the EU's favour.

One could expect that the continuation of the integration process will lead to further development of EU-CEE trade. It will be a factor stimulating an increase in EU foreign trade and thus further improve the EU's balance of trade with the CEE countries. A main condition for the enhancement of mutual benefits, however, could be to counterbalance the EU's trade surplus with an increase in capital outflow to the CEE countries. If this did not materialize, the CEE countries, faced with a rising trade deficit, may be inclined to undertake specific measures to reduce this deficit.

EU fears that an increase of imports from the CEE countries could threaten jobs in member states are unfounded. If the threat was real, it would have manifested itself during the creation of the free trade area. Almost all border regulations applied to CEE industrial goods have already been abolished and EU jobs have not been noticeably affected. Indeed, more exports and job opportunities for EU producers have arisen due to the EU's trade surplus with the CEE countries.

3.4   EU costs of Eastward Enlargement

A number of reports on the costs of enlargement have recently appeared in EU countries, some of which were commissioned by EU institutions. Experts' opinions on the scale of costs vary but some claim enlargement will be too costly for the EU. The standard economic argument against enlargement is that the CEE countries are too poor and too agricultural and they are not yet prepared for membership of a more highly developed EU. It has been argued that the EU simply cannot afford to grant membership to countries of Central and Eastern Europe.[7] Accession of the CEE countries at this time would require big transfers of money from the EU and play havoc with the EU's budget.

Closer analysis of these arguments, however, point more to a pretext for postponing enlargement rather than real barriers to accession. Quite often the arguments employed are exaggerated and are based on incorrect assumptions.[8] For example, among the obstacles to enlargement is the alleged cost of integrating Polish agriculture. The main reasons cited are the fact that farming is an important sector (about 25% of those in work are employed in agriculture) and that the mechanism of the EU's Common Agricultural Policy

(CAP) could not possibly be adjusted to this reality. There is a fear in the EU that integration of Polish agriculture (and of other Central European countries) would involve high budgetary costs which are necessary to support prices of farm products, to finance export refunds, etc. This argument, however, does not take into account that there was a large fall in the volume of agricultural production at the beginning of the 1990s and that the farming structure is such that it is unlikely that rapid expansion of output could occur. 'It is therefore most unlikely that a further liberalization in agricultural trade would have any real significance to agriculture in the Union except in one or two very specific products, which now enjoy high protection (sour cherries, raspberries, etc.).' (Mayhew, 1996, p. 23). Moreover, prices of agricultural products are rising rapidly and in some cases they have already reached or exceeded the world market level, thus making Polish products less competitive internationally.[9] Thus, it seems unlikely that Poland will be in a position to threaten EU farmers in the coming decade or threaten the EU budget.

In the longer run it is probable that farming production will increase significantly and will result in exportable surpluses. By that time, however, further progress in reforming the CAP will have been made as a result of the McSharry reforms and the Uruguay Round results. Both elements should help Poland and the EU deal with the enlargement issue, though most probably they will not be enough.

This is not to say that integrating CEE agriculture into the EU does not present any difficulties. Extending the CAP to those countries certainly is a problem. Agriculture will remain one of the most sensitive issues in future negotiations on membership. The cost of extending that policy to the CEE countries should not, however, be overstated.

One cannot exclude either that some other sectors or regions in the EU may be negatively affected by enlargement. Such costs, however, should be compared with overall benefits accruing to the EU from enlargement. Sectoral or regional threats and resistance against enlargement should not be allowed to stop a process of enlargement. Too much is at stake for all partners involved and for the whole of Europe.

Another common West European argument against accession at this time is that the transition economies must reach an average level of development which is close to that of the EU before they can become full members. The average per capita GDP is lower in the CEE countries than in the EU. One way for the less developed Associated Countries to catch up to the EU is to join the EU and exploit all the benefits of a large market.

Note that when Portugal joined the Community in 1986, its per capita GDP was equal to 32% of the EU average. By 1992 Portugal had improved its position relative to every other member, and the figure stood at 53%. The most likely conclusion is that poor countries have better opportunities to accelerate their development when they are in the Union, not outside. Moreover, 'the desire of Portugal and Ireland and, to a lesser extent of Spain and Italy, not to get left behind in the further process of European integration has boosted their general modernization and growth performance' (de Crombrugghe et al., 1996, p. 4). Certainly, the same incentives are now important for the Associated Countries aiming at full membership of the EU. If the decision on accession or even the length of the transition period is determined by income convergence, a country 'temporarily' excluded may never be able to integrate into the Union.

It is also important to note that GDP levels have never been a formal condition of EU membership in the past and there is no reason to establish more demanding standards for CEE countries than for previous applicants.

One general remark that should be made in the context of discussion on possible consequences of enlargement is that a feature of that debate among experts and politicians is the stress put on the costs of enlargement and, as a result of that, on arguments against Eastward enlargement or at least its postponement. Very few analyses and arguments touch upon the issue of the benefits to the EU of enlargement. EU member states should get a clear picture not only of costs that will arise from enlargement but of its positive consequences as well. Current estimates are restricted to the calculable costs. They should be balanced, however, against long-term positive developments, such as the stabilization of the CEE countries and the strengthening of global competitiveness of an enlarged EU.

There will be some costs to the EU, though they will not be as large as is commonly believed. In this respect it is important to realize that Central and Eastern Europe will not integrate into the EU at once, in one big bloc. Not all CEE countries will be admitted at the same time. EU decisions on new members will depend on many factors, among them on the level of development in individual countries and on corresponding progress in several economic, political and legal fields.

It should also be remembered that previous accession arrangements did not result in displacement of jobs and an inflow of labour from new entrants, as was feared at the time. On the contrary, migratory outflows from the new members diminished as a result of better prospects for employment and economic growth at home.

3.5   Structural Funds

In their present state all the CEE countries would be net beneficiaries of the EU's current structural funds mechanism. Estimates on the transfer of structural funds vary. Even if they amounted to ECU 15 billion—which is roughly the average of various calculations—that would mean that EU member states needed to contribute only an average of 1.48% instead of

1.28% of GDP to the EU budget, which is only an increase by 0.2% of their GDP.[10] This is only a small fraction of the EU's GDP; perhaps political stabilization and increased markets for EU producers and investors are worth this price.

Any realistic assessment of the potential costs of Eastward enlargement related to structural funds also has to take into account the following factors:

- Calculations based on the present transfer mechanism in the EU cannot be used as arguments for the high cost of such transfers because few believe that the EU will retain the current rules of structural funds without changes. It is reasonable to assume that these rules will be changed.
- It is safe to assume that at least part of the structural funds transferred to CEE countries would result in an increase in EU exports to those countries. It has been estimated that up to 46% of structural aid provided to the three poorest members—Greece, Ireland and Portugal—flows back to other member states in the form of export orders. A similar approach would be appropriate with regard to future members of the EU.
- Most structural funds are based on the principle of cofinancing, which means that the applicant country has to contribute to the financing of individual projects—usually up to 50%. It would be unrealistic to assume high transfers to the CEE countries, because interested CEE countries would not have sufficient funds for cofinancing.
- The limited capacity of transition countries to absorb structural funds should be taken into account.

Given the above-mentioned arguments, it is reasonable to expect that transfers of structural funds would not merely be one way, from the EU to the CEE countries; much of these funds would find their way back into the EU in the form of increased imports.

3.6   The Evolution of the EU Position on Enlargement

The Europe Agreements should be seen as important steps towards the reintegration of some CEE countries (or the integration of others) into the Western economic and political system. By signing those Agreements, the European Community reacted quickly and positively to radical political and economic changes set in motion in Central and Eastern Europe in 1989.[11] Despite CEE countries' expectations, the Agreements did not guarantee membership. They contained only unilateral CEE declarations 'recognizing the fact that the final objective of Poland is to become a member of the Community and that this association, in the view of the Parties, will help to achieve this objective' (preamble to the Polish Association Agreement).

The Copenhagen European Council meeting (of EU heads of State and Government) held on 21–22 June 1993 signalled a new phase in the relationship between the Union and the Associated Countries. For the first time the European Council recognized officially that 'the associated countries in Central and Eastern Europe that so desire shall become members of the European Union.'[12] The Copenhagen summit defined the following broad criteria for membership:[13]

(i) the stability of institutions guaranteeing democracy, the rule of law, human rights and respect for the protection of minorities;
(ii) the existence of a functioning market economy and the ability to cope with competitive pressure and market forces within the Union;
(iii) the ability to take on the obligations of membership, including adherence to the aims of political, economic and monetary union.

To facilitate the preparation of the Associated Countries for future membership, the Commission proposed a 'structured dialogue' within a multilateral framework. The essence of the structured relationship was 'the holding of meetings between, on the one hand, the Council of the Union and, on the other hand, all the Associated Countries of Central and Eastern Europe on matters of common interest, decided in advance, arising in the Union's areas of competence' (Mayhew, 1996, p. 14). This high-level political dialogue did not really get started until late 1994, however, and was undertaken only as a result of the conclusions of the Essen summit a year and a half later.

The Essen European Council of December 1994 took a decisive step forward by defining a strategy of pre-accession. This strategy was, at least partly, the result of the Associated Countries' persistent demand that the EU take more concrete steps towards enlargement. The main idea behind the Essen strategy was 'to provide a route plan for the associated countries as they prepare for accession. The essential element of the strategy is their progressive preparation for integration into the internal market of the European Union, through the phased adoption of the Union's internal market *acquis*.... Politically the strategy will be realized through the development of a structured relationship between the associated countries and the Union.' To put it briefly: the strategy's main aim was to help Associated Countries prepare to join the internal market of the Union and to support this process politically by a very extensive multilateral dialogue. Closer cooperation between the EU and the Associated Countries was also provided in a series of areas incorporating all three pillars of the Maastricht Treaty, including common foreign and security policies, and justice and home affairs, i.e., going beyond the internal market issues. It also included environmental protection, joining trans-European networks by Associated Countries, etc.

Following the Council's decisions, the European Commission was asked to draft a White Paper on the preparation of the Associated Countries for integration into the internal market, seen as 'the key element in the strategy to narrow the gap between the applicants and the EU' (European Commission, 1995). This document was released in May and accepted by the Cannes Summit in June 1995. Its aim is to guide the Associated Countries in their preparation to join the internal market, and covers the following three issues.

(i) It lists the internal market *acquis* which is essential in the early stages of preparing for accession. This is not an exhaustive list of all regulations and directives which comprise the legal basis for the internal market, but rather a guide on how to sculpture the main legal framework.
(ii) It suggests a sequence of measures facilitating the adjustment to the internal market directives (i.e., which of them should be introduced in the first stage and which can be applied later).
(iii) It deals with the institutional questions related to the implementation of internal market legislation (how to implement and enforce them effectively).

Poland, like its Central European neighbours, was dissatisfied with the White Paper for at least two reasons. First, the Associated Countries were presented with more stringent conditions than current EU members had to meet, e.g., on environmental standards. Second, the White Paper had omitted some important elements of the accession issue.[14] By focusing on integration into the EU's internal market (and not covering the whole *acquis communautaire*) the White Paper on the internal market was tackling only a part (albeit a substantial part) of the conditions spelt out at the 1994 Essen Summit. Of the 'four freedoms' covered by the Union's internal market, only two are in fact relevant to the pre-accession strategy: trade in goods and movement of capital. There is no mention of the free movement of workers and very little said about trade in services (the supply of some services abroad is directly dependent on the movement of workers).

The EU emphasized several times that the White Paper should not be treated as a list of criteria for judging whether the Associated Countries are ready for accession or not. It is obvious, however, that adjustment to the internal market is one of the main elements of the strategy aimed at preparing the Associated Countries for EU membership.

Despite the existence of a pre-accession strategy and the White Paper, the enlargement process currently still looks unclear (Mayhew, 1996). One reason is the large number of countries applying for EU membership. More important, however, is uncertainty about the direction and scope of changes within the Union itself, making the scenario for enlargement more uncertain than ever (von Ow, 1995). The EU has had to deal with a number of compelling issues, among them the improvement of EU institutions, common policies and decision-making procedures. There are plans to change the structure of future EU budgets and an ambitious programme is under way to create monetary and economic union. All these issues (with the exception of the monetary and economic union) have been tackled at the Inter-Governmental Conference (IGC) launched on 29 March 1996 in Torino, Italy. The agenda and ensuing results of the IGC are of key importance to the EU and crucial to its future.

The IGC is equally important to the Associated Countries. The Union has already made it clear that the start of membership negotiations has to wait until the outcome of the IGC. If the IGC is successful in bringing about an improvement in the efficiency of decision-making processes in the EU, as well as other expected changes, it will have facilitated enlargement. If progress is not made, however, the enlargement will have been made much more difficult.

3.7   Conditions and Timing of Membership

Most observers agree that it is not the EU's Eastern enlargement as such, but its conditions and timing, which are to be decided and which are crucial to the accession issue. As the EU has no moral or political grounds to reject explicitly the accession of the CEE countries, its eventual decision is manifested in the economic criteria it specifies as conditions for accession. 'Conditions that cannot be fulfilled by the candidates, or timing and conditions that are humiliating and thus unacceptable, may effectively block CEE countries' accession without any formal rejection' (Reiter, 1996, p. 2). An extreme case might be to offer so-called 'empty' membership to the CEE countries, i.e., set such peculiar timing and conditions of accession so as to reduce enlargement to a merely symbolic gesture.

One example of this would be a suggestion to exclude agriculture from the membership scheme. Such an idea has already been proposed more or less officially. Another example is the idea of joining the EU, but at first cooperating only in security and political areas, both of which are important to the EU and CEE countries. There is a risk, however, that the EU might use those relatively insensitive areas of cooperation as a pretext to postpone a decision on full membership. Any 'partial' membership is unacceptable for Poland and, most likely, for the other CEE countries. It would deprive them of benefits in the fields in which they have comparative advantage (including agriculture). It would also cause problems for the EU itself. Experts have pointed out that excluding agriculture from the membership scheme would violate the basic rules of the Treaty of Rome and would go against the idea of the single market, as it would undermine the 'integrity' of the EU market (Buckwall et al., 1994).

The EU has already listed some of the conditions of enlargement (among them are the above-mentioned Copenhagen criteria and conditions expressed in the White Paper), and the list could grow longer. One question still open to debate is the range of requirements put forward in the White Paper that have to be implemented by the CEE countries before they become members of the EU. Also, setting a clear date for membership is necessary. Without guarantees as to the timing of accession to the EU, the CEE countries would become increasingly reluctant to bear the high, but necessary, costs of the transformation. Clarification of the timetable for membership would provide a clear picture of changes under way and raise public optimism.

In view of the evolution of the EU position on membership, it is becoming increasingly obvious that the crucial obstacle to the accession of the CEE countries is not so much their capacity to reform but the adaptability of the EU. At the Copenhagen summit in June 1993, the Union's own capacity for enlargement was explicitly cited as a precondition to further enlargement. Thus, the CEE countries face a criterion for accession that they cannot influence; they do not know exactly when and how they can become members of the EU or what type of EU they are likely to join one day.

Thus, necessary conditions should be set for the CEE countries, as well as a precise date for accession when the CEE countries meet those conditions. These would serve as an 'anchor' for the countries aspiring to membership. Transition countries need this type of agreement in order to implement appropriate disciplinary measures in their domestic policies, establish a time-table for the adjustment of laws, accelerate the legislative process, dispel uncertainty about the future, strengthen the confidence of their business communities and encourage additional foreign investment. For the EU, this 'long road ahead' would serve as a constraint on policies and would (hopefully) prevent the EU from further postponing Eastward enlargement.

The CEE countries' prospects for accession are now directly linked to the success of the IGC, whose agenda contains several pending reforms. Given that the implementation of these and other policies is likely to coincide with the start of the third stage of European economic and monetary union, it may be difficult to reach agreement. It is feared that the EU will be so preoccupied with internal reforms that its interest in external problems, such as enlargement, may be reduced. Whatever the case may be, however, the EU must decide whether the Associated Countries should be allowed to join *en bloc* or individually, or in smaller groups. If only some countries are allowed in the first phase, the need to set criteria which would identify which applicants are ready for membership is paramount.

3.8   An Alternative Scenario

The failure to establish a concrete time-table and set of conditions for membership may be harmful to European integration. In other words, '[t]he current ambiguities over EU enlargement court disaster in Europe by upsetting the process of economic and political reforms in the post-Communist economies and by undermining the crucial confidence of investors in the region' (de Crombrugghe et al., 1996, p. 14). Without the prospect of quick membership, the CEE countries might even experience public resistance against integration. This could be the result of having to face increased foreign competition and the threat of continued or even increasing unemployment, while the equivocal assessment of the balance of benefits which to date results from the association with the EU may also arouse hostility. People are usually reluctant to bear the cost and pain of change. They need a decision on membership as a sort of guarantee, an assurance that they will not be deceived by the reform process. Such a decision would also serve as an instrument for further changes and could help to mobilize maximum effort.[15]

Setting a distant, full membership date (for example, beyond the year 2005) would certainly make most CEE countries less willing to accept social and political costs linked to the transition period. Also, other issues, such as monetary union, may become more of a priority to the EU than that of enlargement. As a result, 'second-class' EU members could emerge in Central and Eastern Europe with much smaller potential for integration, but greater potential for conflict (Rosati, 1995, p. 58).

Failing to give the CEE countries a clear idea on EU membership could also have serious negative implications for the European Union. At best it would be a missed opportunity for growth in Western as well as Central Europe. At worse, a failure in the CEE countries could seriously endanger social peace and security in Western Europe not only through illegal migration, but through political unrest, illegal trade in arms and drugs, etc.[16]

3.9   Adjustments Made by CEE Countries

None of the Associated Countries is ready yet for full membership but most of them have made substantial progress in the last few years. The political transformation in the CEE countries is nearly completed. Political changes have become irreversible and the process to create pluralistic civil societies continues to advance.[17] Most CEE countries have made enormous progress over the past seven years, especially in the field of macroeconomic stabilization. Also, some of them have adjusted institutional infrastructure in accordance with EU requirements, including such key areas as the fiscal system, accounting and auditing standards, customs procedures, etc. Certain sectors still requiring fundamental restructuring include agriculture, mining, and some branches of manufacturing, to prepare them to compete with EU producers. More effort is needed also to speed up institutional reforms and legal adjustments.

The CEE countries have to revise thousands of laws to make them compatible with EU regulations. Most of the changes would be necessary anyway in the process of transition to a market economy. A helpful guide in this respect has been the above-mentioned White Paper on adjustments to the internal market. The candidates for accession are not required to assume all directives and other regulations of the internal market immediately, as this would make accession impossible for the foreseeable future. In the course of previous enlargements, interim solutions were repeatedly found for particularly thorny issues. Adjustment periods can go a long way to facilitating accession. It seems, however, that transition periods for individual sectors have to be subject to strict time limits, as lack of transparency could have negative effects and may reduce the pressure for reform on both sides.

Approximation of laws in some areas of the CEE countries' economies is a direct result of the Europe Agreements. The laws include, among others, those on competition, customs, banking and regulations on company accounts and taxes, intellectual property, transportation and the environment. The legal adjustments are seen in the Agreements as one of the most important tasks for the CEE countries. In most CEE countries, work on the approximation of laws covered by the White Paper has already started and is well advanced. The work is taking two main directions: the revision of existing laws and the adoption of new national legislation on the basis of European law. In most CEE countries considerable effort has been made in the area of competition policy. This includes the scaling down and splitting up of former large state enterprises and the liberalization of foreign trade. Each country also attaches great importance to the adjustment of their laws to the EU competition rules, as required by the Europe Agreements.

The Associated Countries are also obliged to improve the protection of intellectual, industrial and commercial property rights in order to provide the level of protection similar to that existing in the EU. Those Associated Countries which are members of the World Trade Organization (the Czech Republic, Hungary, Poland, Romania, Slovakia and Slovenia) have complied with WTO requirements to adjust their domestic legislation to high standards of intellectual rights regulation, as agreed in the Uruguay Round. Similar commitments have been undertaken by EU member states. The upshot is that the Associated Countries are bound to change their domestic laws and make them compatible with international standards set in both the Europe Agreements and multilateral agreements.

In some Associated Countries, legal procedures were adopted to make the harmonization of laws more efficient and soundly based. The Polish government established a procedure[18] that obligates the government to provide each bill with an opinion on its compatibility with EU law. Such an opinion is issued by the Office of the Government's Plenipotentiary for European Integration and Foreign Assistance. In Hungary two resolutions have been passed by the government (2004/1995 and 2174/1995), under which a comprehensive programme was worked out for the harmonization of laws and for the preparation of a separate scheme for the adaptation of these laws to those in the internal market. Under this programme a reference has to be made in all relative bills to the Europe Agreement and to EU legislation.

As indicated previously, the CEE countries have been involved in a structured dialogue with the EU (under the Essen Summit conclusions of December 1994) and many multilateral meetings have taken place since that time within the framework of that dialogue. First, prime ministers of the Associated Countries attended successive meetings of the European Council. Second, some sessions of the Council were attended by the respective ministers of Associated Countries (e.g., ministers of agriculture, justice, home affairs, transport, finance and education). The dialogue aimed to improve understanding of EU problems and give CEE representatives a chance to get acquainted with the workings of the EU and to ease implementation of the necessary changes in their domestic economies.

All CEE countries hope that negotiations on membership start six months after the completion of the IGC. The Madrid Summit's conclusions clearly stated that '[a]ccession negotiations will start simultaneously with all candidate countries.' This does not imply, however, that all negotiations will be completed at the same time. Indeed, as each aspiring EU member has its own specific conditions, stress should be placed on bilateral discussions.[19] This would be a next step in the dialogue between the EU and prospective EU members, which would allow the Commission to prepare its opinions on candidate countries, as required by the conclusions of the Madrid Summit. Such bilateral discussions would offer a unique possibility to build a base for the future accession negotiating teams.

There is no doubt that Poland's bargaining position (as well as that of other Associated Countries) will be fairly weak compared with that of the EU. The enormous asymmetry in mutual importance is evident from any review of relevant statistics. Poland accounted for 2% of EU (12 members) foreign trade in 1994, whereas the EU accounted for 60% of Poland's foreign trade in that year (EU-12) and 70% in 1995 (EU-15). There is also a growing asymmetry in the balance of trade. Apart from these asymmetries, the prevailing contractual framework of Poland-EU relations is unfavourable from Poland's (as well as the other CEE countries') point of view. Although the Europe Agreement constituted a great step forward in Poland's relations with the EU, paradoxically it seriously weakened the country's bargaining position. The main asset that Poland was able to offer was free access for EU exporters to domestic markets. This asset, however, will disappear by the time free trade in industrial goods begins (in 1995 these goods accounted for about 90% of Polish imports from the EU).

Even if negotiations on accession are completed in time, there is likely be a lengthy period of adjustment. Both sides need to specify how long various aspects of adjustment should take. Specific dates (e.g., for the creation of a customs union or the introduction of common policies) were set up earlier by the EU. The CEE countries also need a clear time-table for the solution of transitional problems as it would help mobilize people and encourage them to work harder. If the EU is indecisive in its approach, the whole process of Poland's integration into the Union will be slower and the Union's position less credible.

Some of the CEE countries are members of the WTO. Adjusting to WTO requirements concerning the liberalization of trade in goods and services on a global scale will help those Central European WTO members to adjust to EU rules and norms, as the EU has to make its regulatory system fully compatible with WTO requirements as well.

3.10   The Need for Reform Within the EU

The EU also needs reforms, among which are changing institutions and common EU policies to accommodate the increased number of members, and drawing up a single set of rules of behaviour for all member states. These issues are under discussion within the framework of the IGC. Changes must also be made in the regulations governing the flow of goods and services. The EU has to accept that producers in the CEE countries are and will remain competitive in many products which are neither subsidized nor sold at prices which are below the cost of production.

Delaying reforms in sensitive sectors in the EU will result in increasingly higher costs to the Union's budget and its taxpayers. Agriculture is a case in point. It would be difficult for the Union to absorb the difficulties an unreformed Common Agricultural Policy (CAP) would pose to accession. In the absence of further reform, the burden the CAP imposes on the EU budget would be substantial, although estimates of this burden differ widely. The last reform, undertaken in 1992, was insufficient. Yet, in the final analysis the precise costs are not decisive. Agriculture is now less heavily regulated and subsidized in Poland than in the EU and the country is making efforts to create and extend market institutions. In contrast to widely-held expectations, Poland has a trade deficit with the EU in agricultural goods as a result of consumer preferences and EU export refunds. Thus, the lack of progress in implementing reforms within the EU brings with it the danger that market reforms already undertaken in Poland's farming sector will be reversed (Weise, 1995, p. 19). A reform of EU agricultural policy must seek to reduce further the distortions emanating from the price mechanisms and artificial production incentives. To the extent that a reduction in the level of price intervention requires that measures be taken to avoid social hardship, the financial responsibility for such measures should be returned to the member states (see Tangermann et al., 1994).

3.11   Spontaneous Integration

In the course of the transition process, CEE countries' foreign trade has already been reoriented towards the EU to a large extent. This reorientation was partly related to the transformation process and the collapse of the CMEA, but also to the normalization of ties following a period in which economic cooperation was distorted for political reasons. Speedy, positive changes occurred at the beginning of the 1990s. The EU has become the main trading partner of all CEE countries, although the EU's share of trade differs from country to country. In 1994, among the six Central European countries (Bulgaria, Czech Republic, Hungary, Poland, Romania and Slovakia) the EU (12 members) was the most important partner for Poland, receiving 63% of Poland's exports, and the least important for Bulgaria, with 34%. (At the same time, these six CEE countries accounted for less than 2% of EU trade in 1989, increasing to 5.7% in 1994.)

The way trade ties between the CEE countries and the EU have developed, however, is in some respects worrisome. While the Europe Agreements were aimed at helping the CEE countries in their recovery by opening up export markets, their objectives have not been fully achieved. The opening of EU markets to the CEE countries has in some cases resulted in very moderate or even empty concessions for the following reasons.

(i)   The process of elimination of EU barriers against CEE products was the longest for goods of greatest importance to those countries. Agriculture— a key CEE export sector—benefited little because of a limited reduction of barriers.

(ii) The EU has at times offered concessions on products which are not exported by the CEE countries (for example, microwave ovens benefit from duty-free ceilings under Poland's Europe Agreement).

Despite EU preferences in access to its markets, all CEE countries have registered trade deficits with the EU (since 1991) and these are also likely to increase. In the CEE countries, exports which ought to benefit from the opening of the EU markets were growing, but usually at a slower pace than imports, even though the CEE countries started to open their markets to EU products at a later stage (based on the principle of asymmetry). Even in agricultural and food, the CEE countries started to import more goods from the EU than they exported. (Subsidized) EU products began replacing local products which are no longer competitive since CEE subsidies were drastically cut during transition (mainly as a result of budgetary constraints but also as part of economic reforms). It must be remembered, however, that foreign trade is affected by several different factors and it is impossible to say to what extent exports responded to EU liberalization and why trade deficits have appeared. Limited and modest EU liberalization was only one of the reasons for the deficits (see Kawecka-Wyrzykowska, 1995). In any case, decision-makers in the CEE countries have problems in explaining to their domestic constitutencies why they have trade deficits with the EU.

3.12 Changing Social Attitudes

An important element of the integration process is the social acceptance of EU membership in the CEE countries. A survey published for the EU in Central and Eastern Europe (Eurobarometer No. 6) shows that on average 90% of people in the Associated Countries are in favour of EU membership. Estonia is the least enthusiastic, with 76% in favour, followed by the Czech Republic (76%), Hungary (80%), Latvia (80%), Bulgaria (86%), Lithuania (86%), Slovakia (88%), Poland (93%) and Romania (97%).

Since the Eurobarometer survey of November 1994, however, the EU's image has become less positive in each of these countries, except in Poland where it has improved by four percentage points. Support for EU membership is thus still high but it is diminishing in almost all CEE countries, and indeed could even dry up. At a time when the CEE countries have to struggle with the negative effects of transition (for example, high unemployment which is still rising) and competition from foreign goods is getting tougher, there is a risk that the people in the CEE countries start to perceive EU membership as risky and withdraw most of their current support. A wave of 'Euro-scepticism' in the CEE countries could also undermine the impetus for integration in the European Union.

3.13 Regional Cooperation

After the dissolution of the CMEA in the summer of 1991 and the collapse of regional trade at the beginning of the 1990s, 1994 was the first year in which trade among the CEE countries recovered strongly. This trend continued into 1995, especially among Central European Free Trade Agreement (CEFTA) countries. Nevertheless, the weight of intra-group trade in total CEE trade remains relatively small. Exports by CEFTA countries to other CEFTA member in 1995 varied between 5% of total exports in Poland and Slovenia to 8% of total exports in Slovakia and the Czech Republic (excluding trade between the Czech Republic and Slovakia).

Institutional cooperation is also weak, even within the framework of CEFTA. This situation partly reflects a negative experience of mutual cooperation in the past and is partly related to a 'race' for admission into the EU. The latter is probably based on an assumption that each country can obtain EU membership faster on an individual, rather than collective, basis.

One should not expect a significant increase in the importance of mutual trade among the CEE countries at the expense of other partners (for example, the EU). This is not because of the inability of CEE countries to cooperate among themselves but because of some very practical considerations. Strong and sustained economic growth in the CEE countries requires modernization. All these countries are interested in buying advanced technologies and manufactured goods to restructure their economies. The main anchor for modernization, however, is the EU, not the CEE countries. Therefore, the future of regional cooperation in Central and Eastern Europe depends to a large extent on the pace and quality of changes in CEE trade with the EU as well. Also, some CEE countries are heavily in debt to the West. This factor is an impetus to develop exports to creditor countries. Some CEE countries have well-established and long-lasting relations with Germany or France or other Western countries. A higher level of regional economic and trade cooperation among CEE countries will be the result of successful integration into the global economy, and first of all, of joining the EU, not *vice versa*.

As it is, there are several examples of cooperation among the CEE countries, one of which is CEFTA. The pace of trade liberalization has been faster under CEFTA (especially for agricultural products) than under the Europe Agreements. It has attracted membership of other countries from the region (Slovenia joined in 1996), and Lithuania, Bulgaria and Romania have expressed an interest in joining.

Active participation of most CEE countries in other regional and multilateral initiatives also contradicts the idea that these countries are not yet ready for mutual cooperation. Such initiatives include the Central European Initiative, membership or negotiations on membership of the WTO (for the whole region) and membership of some CEE countries in the OECD. These initiatives show that the CEE countries are ready and able to make far-reaching adjustments in domestic laws to be eligible to cooperate with international organizations and other countries.

3.14   Concluding Remarks

– The real process of CEE countries joining the EU in political and economic areas is already under way. The EU has become the main trading partner of all CEE countries.
– In order to give CEE countries equal opportunities to compete with the EU suppliers, all subsidies for EU agricultural exports to CEE countries should be suspended until these countries become members of the Union.
– Many CEE countries have already taken steps to comply with the *acquis communautaire*. Some countries have already implemented rules providing for compulsory harmonization of their domestic laws with the laws of the EU.

- The present Europe Agreements on association are not sufficient to maximize benefits of cooperation and to support the process of transformation in the CEE countries. Concrete deadlines and time-tables are needed to give these countries a clear perspective on membership of the European Union. Failure to set precise dates on membership makes the EU's commitment towards enlargement vague. In this situation, accession may be easily postponed.
- From the CEE countries' point of view, the real question is when and how accession will take place, not whether it should come about.
- The EU's decision on enlargement should be rapid and subject to clear conditions. It does not necessarily mean an immediate granting of membership. In some areas, longer adjustment periods will be necessary. In any case, a speedy decision would be optimal, as it would mobilize CEE efforts to achieve accession as well as help to organize the necessary adjustments. The objective of EU membership remains the most important incentive to keep political and economic reform in the Associated Countries on course, despite the high social costs.
- Postponement of enlargement would have a negative economic impact on the CEE countries in that uncertainty discourages investors, foreign and domestic. Uncertainty over enlargement may also upset the process of economic and political reforms in the CEE countries.
- Failure to give the CEE countries a clear idea of when and how EU membership will be granted could also have negative implications for the European Union, in that it might seriously endanger security in Western Europe through illegal immigration, illegal trade in arms, etc. It would also prolong the continuation of the division of Europe.
- Accession to the EU is important not only for Poland and the Union but for the whole of Europe, which would gain from the process politically and economically. It would create greater security and stability, and more economic cooperation and thus increased growth.
- More detailed studies are needed on the possible consequences of enlargement. It is difficult to put forward precise estimates on the overall budgetary effects of enlargement, particularly because of the still uncertain results of the IGC, the development of EU policies and the pace of change in the CEE countries. New estimates which would help towards deciding on the length of adjustment of individual sectors, and thus on a strategy which would incur the least costs, are also needed.
- Some EU officials and Western authors seem to prefer the idea of offering Union membership in only some areas (mainly those which the EU does not consider sensitive, such as security and political cooperation), and excluding new members from other areas of vital importance. The two main suggestions put forward have been membership without the full integration of the agricultural sector or without financial transfers. This

approach, which is unacceptable to the CEE countries, would increase and not reduce the asymmetry of benefits, to the advantage of the EU. Enlargement must not lead to second-class treatment of the CEE countries.
– Enlargement should not be seen as a difficult obstacle but as a challenge. It is up to both the EU and CEE countries to meet this challenge. The CEE countries, however, feel increasingly frustrated that the EU requires of them increasingly greater efforts to reform, whereas it is reluctant to make important decisions on the timing and conditions of accession.

What is at stake is the adjustment of the whole of Europe to the post-Cold War era: the integration of a divided Europe to prevent future conflicts and achieve maximum possible benefits from international cooperation. This will require a mutual adjustment of the CEE countries and the EU to a future common Europe.

Notes

* The author gratefully acknowledges the helpful comments from Stefan Kawalec and Lesław Paga. The views expressed in this paper are those of the author.
  1. This paper is based mainly on the author's knowledge of Poland's experience and its approach towards the issue of EU membership. It addresses, however, the problems of enlargement facing all Associated Countries of Central and Eastern Europe. In certain areas the position of other CEE countries may be different from Poland's.
  2. The term 'CEE countries' (Central and Eastern European countries) covers the ten countries which have already signed Europe Agreements on their association with the EU.
  3. For more on the assessment of Poland's Europe Agreement see Kawecka-Wyrzykowska (1995).
  4. It is worth noting here that the premise of West European integration was originally political. The first institution of an integrative nature—the European Coal and Steel Community—was set up to prevent the re-emergence of German militarism and to draw Germany into the broad framework of European integration. That policy proved to be successful and is an example worth remembering in the Europe of the 1990s.
  5. A similarly positive outcome has also followed Poland's and some other CEE countries' joining the World Trade Organization and far-reaching commitments undertaken by those countries within the Uruguay Round of negotiations. See Kawecka-Wyrzykowska (1994).
  6. Source: Eurostat.
  7. This is a change from earlier days. According to former Spanish Prime Minister Felipe Gonzalez, 'Ten years ago, EU leaders would have gladly paid 1% of GDP to knock down the Berlin Wall, end the separation of Europe, get rid of communism and dictatorships and bring about the prospect of a politically united Europe. Now nobody accepts that it may cost even 0.2% more of GDP. Enlargement will cost money, but much less than is said, and much more spread out over time…' Interview in the *Financial Times*, 6 December 1995.
  8. Also see D. Rosati (1995).
  9. It is also necessary to point out the limits placed on agricultural production resulting from the Uruguay Round agreement, and thus the lower support that may be required for CEE agriculture. One might argue that the Uruguay Round agreement on agriculture, which has imposed limits on all forms of protection in this sector and thus limited production, was a good opportunity to make changes in the Common Agricultural Policy (CAP).
  10. This estimate was calculated by the Keil Institute of World Economics, cited in Stehn, J. (1994), 'Stufen einer Osterweiterung der Europaeischen Union', *Die Weltwirtschaft*, No. 2.
  11. Earlier signs of support from the EC and of positive changes in its trade policy towards the CEE countries were the suspension of quantitative restrictions applied until then on some products coming from CEE countries; inclusion of the CEE countries in the GSP; and

launching the PHARE programme. All those measures were applied first only to Poland and Hungary, the two countries which started the transformation, and were subsequently extended to the other CEE countries.

12. 'The New Phase in Relations', *Together in Europe*, No. 32, 1 July 1993, p. 1. The European Council also recognized the crucial importance of trade in the transition countries, and approved the additional concessions to the Associated Countries which facilitated a faster opening of the EU market for products coming from the Associated Countries than it was envisaged in the original Europe Agreements.

13. In addition, the European Council underlined that accession would depend on the capacity of the Union to take on new members while maintaining the momentum of European integration.

14. A. Mayhew points to an additional element that is of crucial importance to the Associated Countries. He writes that the White Paper 'goes beyond what an unbiased observer would consider good for the economic development of... [the Associated Countries] and strays into social and environmental directives which are clearly aimed at reducing these countries' ability to compete with producers in the Union. No doubt this will be ignored by the associated countries when they draw up their own individual White Papers' (Mayhew, 1996, p. 32). L. Orlowski (1995, p. 45) underlines that '[G]iven limited EU social safety standards and rules, the Visegrad group countries have no clear direction for legislative adjustments.'

15. De Crombrugghe, Minton-Beddoes and Sachs refer in their paper to recent developments in economic theory to show the importance of a clearer commitment to enlargement. They argue that by offering a credible time-table for membership, the European Union can coordinate the expectations of agents in Central Europe, and of potential foreign investors, towards a high-investment (high-growth) equilibrium. The time horizon over which accession is expected to occur will affect the credibility of the commitment. Moreover, they stress that the discipline of the EU's legal framework and its enforcement institutions offers guarantees of a reliable economic environment. See de Crombrugghe et al. (1996), p. 3.

16. This argument is stressed, among others, by de Crombrugghe et al. (1996), p. 5.

17. For more on the specific conditions facing individual CEE countries see Weidenfeld (1995).

18. Under the Government Ordinance of 29 March 1994. Moreover, following a request from the Polish parliament in 1992, all Government has been preparing yearly reports on the progress of the implementation of all commitments inscribed in the Europe Agreement. The last report was discussed and approved by parliament in March 1996.

19. This proposal was put forward by Poland's President A. Kwaśniewski during his meeting in Brussels with the European Commission's President J. Santer on 18 January 1996 (see, 'Together in Europe', No. 82, 1 February 1996).

References

Buch, P. (1995): 'East-West Economic Cooperation. Interests Involved, Institutional Possibilities and Economic Rationale', *Intereconomics* 30.

Buckwell, A. et al. (1994): 'Feasibility of an agricultural strategy to prepare the countries of Central and Eastern Europe for EU accession', *Report for Directorate General I of EC*, Brussels.

De Crombrugghe, A., Minton-Beddoes, Z. and Sachs, J. D. (1996): 'EU Membership for Central Europe. Commitments, Speed and Conditionality', Facultes Universitaires Notre-Dame de la Paix.

European Commission (1995): 'Preparation of the Associated Countries of Central and Eastern Europe for Integration into the Internal Market of the Union', White Paper, Brussels, 3 May 1995, COM (95) 163, final, 2 vols.

Inotai, A. (1993): 'The Economic Impacts of the Association Agreement: The Case of Hungary', Working Paper No. 16, Institute for World Economics, Budapest.

Kawecka-Wyrzykowska, E. (1994): 'The Impact of the Positive Conclusion of the Uruguay Round on Intraregional Trade with Special Reference to the Countries in Transition', Economic Commission for Europe, Trade/R619.

Kawecka-Wyrzykowska, E. (1995): 'Association Agreements and Central Europe's Trade with the European Union: Poland', in K. Mizsei and A. Rudka (eds.), *From Association to Accession*, Warsaw, Prague, Budapest, Kosice, New York, The Windsor Group and Institute for EastWest Studies, pp. 15–52.

Mayhew, A. (1996): 'Going beyond the Europe Agreements: The European Union's Strategy for Accession', in F. Franzmeyer and C. Weise (eds.), *Poland und die Osterweiterung der Europaeischen Union*, Berlin, Duncker and Humboldt.

Orlowski, L. (1995): 'Social Safety Nets in Central Europe: Preparation for Accession to the European Union', *Comparative Economic Studies* 37.

Reiter, S. (1996): 'Eastern Enlargement of the European Union from a Western and Eastern Perspective', Research Reports No. 227, *Wiener Institute fuer Internationale Wirtschaftsvergleiche*.

Rosati, D. (1995): 'Impediments to Poland's Accession to the European Union: Real or Imaginary?', in E. Kawecka-Wyrzykowska and T. Roe (eds.), *Polish Agriculture and Enlargement of the European Union*, Warsaw School of Economics, pp. 51–64.

Tangerman, S., Josling, T. (1994): 'Pre-accession Agricultural Policies for Central Europe and the European Union', final report, study commissioned by the European Commission.

Von Ow, B. (1995): 'The accession of the countries of Central and Eastern Europe into the European Union: problems and perspectives', in W. Weidenfeld (ed.), *Central and Eastern Europe on the Way into the European Union*, Guetersloh, Bertelsmann Foundation Publishers.

Weidenfeld, W. (ed.) (1995): *Central and Eastern Europe on the Way into the European Union*, Guetersloh, Bertelsmann Foundation Publishers.

Weise, C. (1995): 'Poland's Path to the European Union', *Economic Bulletin* 32:12, German Institute for Economic Research, December.

Index